DORLING KINDERSLEY 📖 EYEWITNESS BOOKS

REPTILE

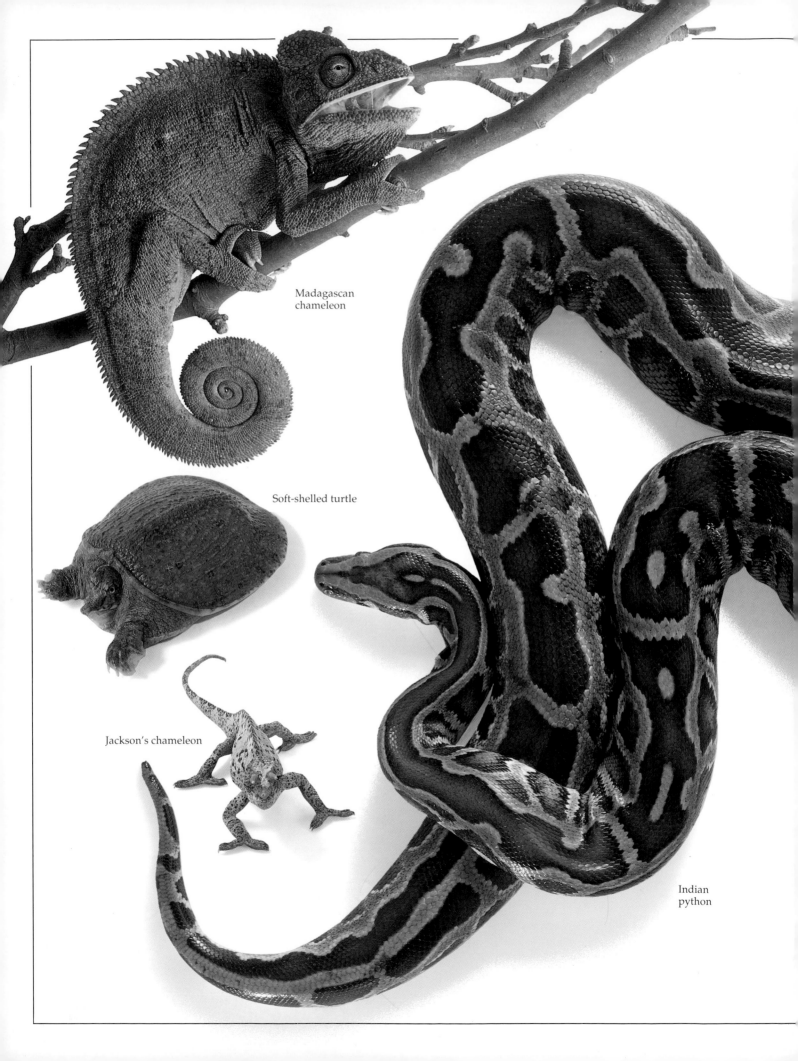

Madagascan
chameleon

Soft-shelled turtle

Jackson's chameleon

Indian
python

DK EYEWITNESS BOOKS

Starred tortoise

Radiated tortoise

REPTILE

Written by
COLIN McCARTHY

Sinaloan milk snake

Basilisk lizard

Red-eared terrapin

Caiman

Eyed lizard

DK
Dorling Kindersley

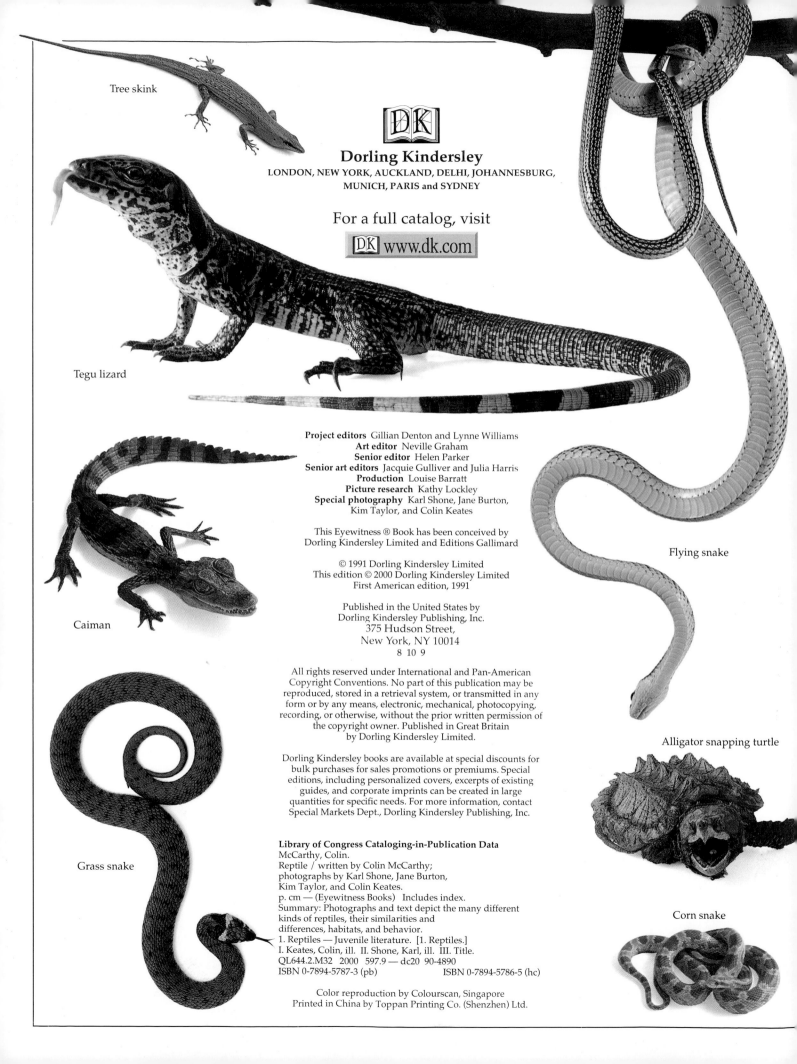

Tree skink

DK

Dorling Kindersley

LONDON, NEW YORK, AUCKLAND, DELHI, JOHANNESBURG,
MUNICH, PARIS and SYDNEY

For a full catalog, visit

DK www.dk.com

Tegu lizard

Flying snake

Project editors Gillian Denton and Lynne Williams
Art editor Neville Graham
Senior editor Helen Parker
Senior art editors Jacquie Gulliver and Julia Harris
Production Louise Barratt
Picture research Kathy Lockley
Special photography Karl Shone, Jane Burton,
Kim Taylor, and Colin Keates

This Eyewitness ® Book has been conceived by
Dorling Kindersley Limited and Editions Gallimard

© 1991 Dorling Kindersley Limited
This edition © 2000 Dorling Kindersley Limited
First American edition, 1991

Published in the United States by
Dorling Kindersley Publishing, Inc.
375 Hudson Street,
New York, NY 10014
8 10 9

Caiman

Dorling Kindersley books are available at special discounts for
bulk purchases for sales promotions or premiums. Special
editions, including personalized covers, excerpts of existing
guides, and corporate imprints can be created in large
quantities for specific needs. For more information, contact
Special Markets Dept., Dorling Kindersley Publishing, Inc.

Alligator snapping turtle

Library of Congress Cataloging-in-Publication Data
McCarthy, Colin.
Reptile / written by Colin McCarthy;
photographs by Karl Shone, Jane Burton,
Kim Taylor, and Colin Keates.
p. cm — (Eyewitness Books) Includes index.
Summary: Photographs and text depict the many different
kinds of reptiles, their similarities and
differences, habitats, and behavior.
1. Reptiles — Juvenile literature. [1. Reptiles.]
I. Keates, Colin, ill. II. Shone, Karl, ill. III. Title.
QL644.2.M32 2000 597.9 — dc20 90-4890
ISBN 0-7894-5787-3 (pb)   ISBN 0-7894-5786-5 (hc)

Grass snake

Corn snake

Color reproduction by Colourscan, Singapore
Printed in China by Toppan Printing Co. (Shenzhen) Ltd.

Contents

Rat snake

What is a reptile?

THERE ARE FOUR GROUPS of reptiles alive today: turtles and tortoises, snakes and lizards, the crocodile family, and the tuatara. Reptiles, like fish, amphibians, birds, and mammals are vertebrates (they have backbones), and their young are usually born on land. When reptiles hatch from their eggs, they look like mini-versions of their parents. Reptiles have scaly skin, which is good at keeping in body moisture, so they can live in dry places. The skin is less successful at keeping in body heat. Therefore, reptiles depend on their surroundings for warmth. Although considered cold-blooded, the blood of a sun-warmed reptile is about the same temperature as ours. Warm-blooded creatures have to eat often to maintain their body temperature, and use up energy looking for food. Reptiles do not need to eat to keep warm and so survive well in barren areas.

Scaly skin

DREAMY DRAGONS
Reptiles have featured in the mythology of many countries for hundreds of years. The dragons illustrated here were described by Marco Polo, the famous Italian explorer, who had possibly seen huge species of lizards and snakes on his travels. The winged dragons were probably inspired by flying lizards he had seen in the far east. The evil multi-headed hydra grew two heads when one was cut off. In Greek legend, Hercules finally killed the beast by burning each neck as the head was cut off.

Hydra

Extra-long toe for added support

What is not a reptile?

At first glance, the salamander looks like a lizard, however, it is not a reptile but an amphibian. Amphibians, for example frogs and toads, are often mistaken for reptiles, though they belong to a different class of animals. Amphibians are unlike reptiles in many ways. They have no scales and breathe through their skin. The skin is kept moist by special mucus glands. Most frogs, toads, and salamanders need to be near water when they breed. They often lay their eggs in water, where the tadpoles then hatch. This European fire salamander, however, keeps her eggs inside her body until seconds before hatching, when she gives birth to live tadpoles directly into the water.

Fire salamander

Like all frogs, this monkey frog is an amphibian. Unlike reptiles, most frogs have smooth, moist skin and no scales.

External ear

Tail helps balance

Eye with movable eyelid

Many reptiles have special tongues

TEGU LIZARD
Reptiles come in all sorts of shapes and sizes. Lizards are one of the biggest and most varied groups. Tegu lizards come from tropical South America. This is a young tegu, but as tegus age, they get fatter from their diet of young birds, mammals, and even other lizards. The tegu's skin is covered with horny, dead scales which are good at keeping in the body's fluids. The tegu's eyelids are movable like most other lizards. However, some geckos, and most snakes, cannot blink, as their eyes are protected by a solid, transparent window. The feet of many reptiles give a good clue to the animals' life-style. They may be used for clambering over smooth surfaces, climbing among swaying stems, or negotiating hot, soft sand dunes. Some burrowing lizards, and most snakes, have no legs.

LAYING ON LAND
Most reptiles lay eggs (pp. 20–21), though some give birth to live young. Unlike most amphibians, reptiles lay their eggs on land including the reptiles which normally spend a great deal of their life in water, such as turtles and crocodiles. Reptiles lay their eggs in a great variety of sites – in sand, in grass, on riverbanks, and in termite mounds. The incubation period is different for each species and is affected by climate.

African grass snake with eggs

When reptiles ruled the world

PTEROSAURS
Flying reptiles, or pterosaurs, dominated the air for over 100 million years, until they became extinct at the same time as the dinosaurs. Their wings were membranes stretched between a single long finger and their legs.

Tʜᴇ ꜰɪʀꜱᴛ ʀᴇᴘᴛɪʟᴇꜱ ᴀᴘᴘᴇᴀʀᴇᴅ some 340 million years ago during the time known as the Carboniferous period. They evolved from amphibians, and although not much is known of their very early history, it seems likely that these first reptiles looked like some of our lizards today. It was not until the later Mesozoic era, 230 to 70 million years ago, that flying reptiles appeared. During this period other reptiles gave up living on land and returned to dominate the seas and lakes, and dinosaurs ruled the land. The reptiles owe their success mainly to their special eggs (pp. 6–7), which, unlike those of amphibians, usually have shells, and do not need to be laid in water. Reptiles themselves were therefore more adaptable and able to live in habitats which would be unsuitable for water-dependent amphibians.

Vertebra of *Palaeophis*, an ancient sea snake

ANCIENT GIANTS
The enormous vertebrae of an extinct form of sea snake, known as *Palaeophis*, found in West Africa, proved the existence in the Cenozoic era of a snake three to four times the size of a modern python. The vertebra shown here is from a present-day python over 20 ft (6 m) long. Though stories of 65 ft (20 m) long ancient snakes have been reported, such creatures are probably mythical.

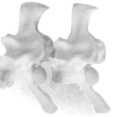

Vertebra of a modern python

TIME CHART OF THE EARTH (Millions of years ago)

Paleozoic era		Mesozoic era			Cenozoic era
Carboniferous period	Permian period	Triassic period	Jurassic period	Cretaceous period	Palaeocene period to the present day
350	270	225	190	141	70
	Turtles, tortoises, and terrapins				
		Crocodilians			
		Lizards			
				Snakes	

Duration of each period not to scale

SLOW TO CHANGE
Lizards first appeared about 200 million years ago, evolving alongside dinosaurs. Although rarely found as fossils, there is evidence that different lizards existed before the end of the Mesozoic era. This example, which is 190 million years old, shows the small head, short neck, long body and tail, and sprawling legs that are still typical of the group today.

Pointed teeth for eating fish

OLD CROCS
The crocodile is probably the closest living relative of dinosaurs and seems to have evolved at the same time, during the Triassic period, about 200 million years ago. The sharp, pointed teeth of early crocodiles suggest that they were mostly specialized fish-eaters, unlike most modern species, which sometimes eat plants along with their meat. The basic crocodile skull has changed little.

Ancient crocodile skull

DOG-JAW

This skull with its doglike jaws belonged to a meat-eating reptile called *Cynognathus*. This four-footed creature was an advanced form of the mammal-like reptiles, which dominated land animals through much of the Permian and Triassic periods. It was from this group of reptiles that mammals evolved about 195 million years ago.

A reconstruction of an advanced mammal-reptile showing an improved non-sprawling posture

Strong jaw and large teeth for meat-eating

Skull of *Cynognathus*

TURTLE FIRST

The fossilized remains of the first recognizable turtle were found in rocks some 200 million years old. Although never one of the dominating reptiles, the turtle's structure was flexible enough to cope with the many changes in the environment that have taken place since it evolved. This adaptability has allowed turtles to develop successful land and aquatic forms, and to become the oldest living group of reptiles.

TOOTHLESS

The skull of a modern turtle has no roof openings, and there are no teeth in the jaws (pp. 32–33). The skull of *Proganochelys*, which dates from the early Triassic period, shows that the top of the skull has not changed. There are, however, toothlike projections in the roof of the mouth, although they are not visible here.

Toothless jaws

9

Happy families

EVOLUTION IS THE BASIS for the classification of animals. In the same way that you are related to your brothers and sisters because you share the same parents, and to your cousins because you share the same grandparents, animals are divided up into family groups according to their common ancestors. Lizards and snakes, therefore, are more closely related to each other than to any other group, but surprisingly, crocodiles are more closely related to birds than to other reptiles. However, because there is often not enough evidence about ancestors, family groupings also depend on the common features of the animals alive today (pp. 6–7).

REPTILES TODAY
Only four groups of reptiles have managed to survive until modern times. The largest by far are the lizards and the snakes. The others were not always so scarce; fossils of at least 108 species of crocodilians have been found, and the group to which the tuatara belongs was at one time also made up of many more species.

	Lizards 3,000 species
	Snakes 2,700 species
	Turtles 200 species
	Crocodilians 23 species
	Tuatara 2 species

Monitor lizard

LIZARDS
Lizards come in many different shapes and sizes. Iguanas, agamas, and chameleons are closely related to each other, and together with geckos form the most primitive lizard group. Girdle-tail lizards, skinks, wall and sand lizards, and whiptails and racerunners are another closely related group. Monitors, beaded lizards, and glass lizards are also grouped together (pp. 28–29).

DAVID AND GOLIATH
The largest reptile in the world is the estuarine or saltwater crocodile. It is an aggressive crocodile and commonly grows to a length of 16 ft (5 m) but specimens as long as 26 ft (8 m) have been recorded. It is found from southern India to northern Australia. The smallest reptile in the world is the British Virgin Island gecko, which is often no longer than 0. 7 in (18 mm).

British Virgin Island gecko

Estuarine crocodile

SNAKES

Snakes are legless reptiles with long, slender bodies. There are three groups of snakes: primitive snakes, which include pythons and boas; blind snakes, which include thread snakes; and advanced snakes, which include rear-fanged snakes, cobras, sea snakes, and vipers. Snakes are found all over the world except in very cold areas (pp. 26–27).

Indian python

TURTLES

Turtles are reptiles with short, broad bodies enclosed in a bony shell. The bone of the shell is usually covered by horny plates, or less commonly, by leathery skin. Turtles are divided into two main groups: hidden-neck turtles, which retract the head and neck into the shell in a vertical S-shaped curve (these include snapping turtles, terrapins, tortoises, sea turtles, and softshell turtles); and side-necked turtles, which bend the neck to the side and hide it under the lip of the shell (these include the snake-necked turtle, the matamata, and African mud turtles).

Hermann's tortoise

CROCODILIANS

Crocodilians are divided into three families: crocodiles, gavials, and alligators, which includes caimans. They are a very old group of reptiles but in several ways are more advanced than the other groups. They have a much more efficient circulatory system, and according to some, are more intelligent. They also are more attentive to their young (pp. 34–35).

Caiman

Inside out

IN MANY REPTILES, bone growth does not stop at maturity, which means that some reptiles keep growing throughout their lives. If a reptile survives the everyday dangers of life, it may eventually become giant-sized. This is particularly true of pythons, crocodiles, and giant tortoises, though smaller lizards and turtles usually stop growing after they reach a certain size. Also, most reptiles do not lose their teeth when they are old, as mammals do; they shed the old teeth and grow new ones (pp. 38–39).

Tail vertebra

Trunk vertebra

Unlike a snake, the insides of a lizard are symmetrical (even)

Chameleon skeleton

Skull

Ribs

CHAMELEON
Many lizards have highly specialized skeletons. The chameleon, for example, is adapted for life in trees and bushes. The body is broad, providing greater stability when the animal's weight is centered over a narrow twig or branch (pp. 28–29). The fingers and toes are designed for grasping. Each hind leg has three toes on the outside and two on the inside, and each foreleg has just the opposite. The tail is prehensile, that is, tailor-made for grasping.

CAIMAN
The caiman's skull is long, and the eye sockets and nostrils are set high. In this way, the caiman can float with just its nose and eyes above the water. Its body is long too. It has two pairs of short legs, and the toes – five on the front feet and four on the back – are partly webbed. The upper jaw of the caiman, as is true of all other members of the crocodile family, is almost solid bone.

Caiman skeleton

Skull

Neck vertebra

Tail vertebra

Ribs

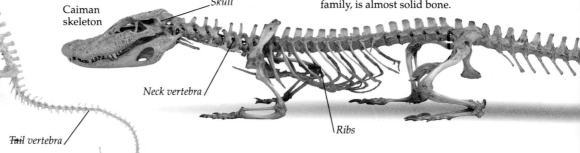

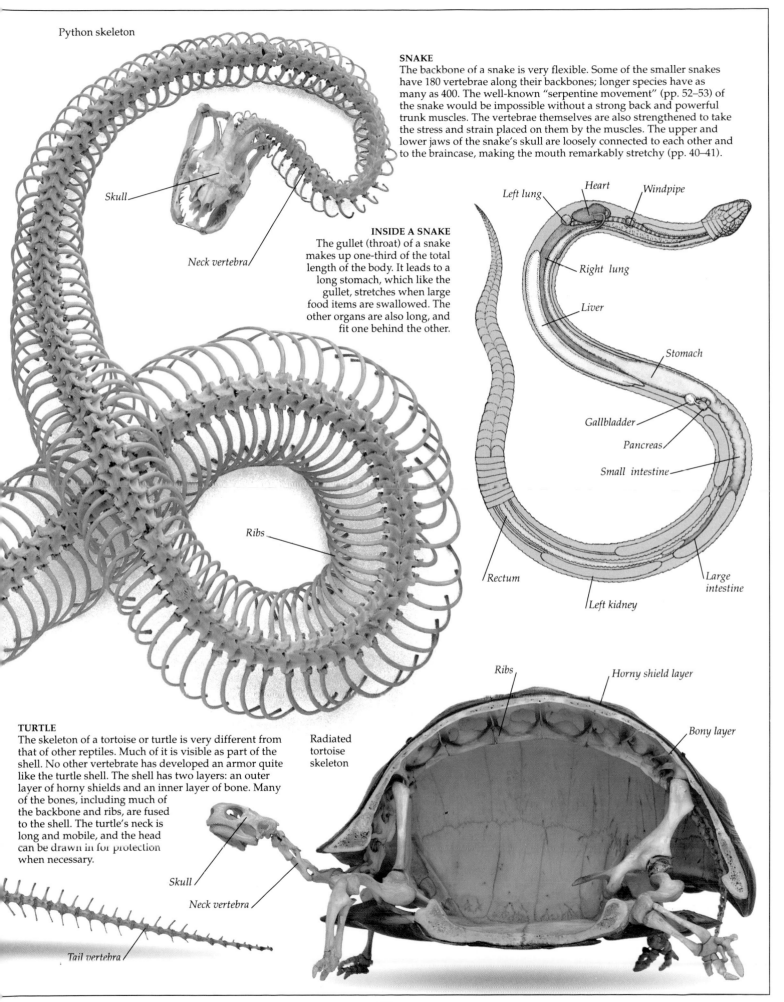

Python skeleton

Skull

Neck vertebra

Ribs

SNAKE

The backbone of a snake is very flexible. Some of the smaller snakes have 180 vertebrae along their backbones; longer species have as many as 400. The well-known "serpentine movement" (pp. 52–53) of the snake would be impossible without a strong back and powerful trunk muscles. The vertebrae themselves are also strengthened to take the stress and strain placed on them by the muscles. The upper and lower jaws of the snake's skull are loosely connected to each other and to the braincase, making the mouth remarkably stretchy (pp. 40–41).

INSIDE A SNAKE

The gullet (throat) of a snake makes up one-third of the total length of the body. It leads to a long stomach, which like the gullet, stretches when large food items are swallowed. The other organs are also long, and fit one behind the other.

Left lung

Heart

Windpipe

Right lung

Liver

Stomach

Gallbladder

Pancreas

Small intestine

Large intestine

Rectum

Left kidney

Ribs

Horny shield layer

Bony layer

TURTLE

The skeleton of a tortoise or turtle is very different from that of other reptiles. Much of it is visible as part of the shell. No other vertebrate has developed an armor quite like the turtle shell. The shell has two layers: an outer layer of horny shields and an inner layer of bone. Many of the bones, including much of the backbone and ribs, are fused to the shell. The turtle's neck is long and mobile, and the head can be drawn in for protection when necessary.

Radiated tortoise skeleton

Skull

Neck vertebra

Tail vertebra

Cool customers

REPTILES ARE COLD-BLOODED (pp. 6–7). This means that their temperature changes with that of their surroundings. It takes time for them to adjust to rapid temperature changes, so they live best where the climate is usually hot. To speed the process of warming, a reptile will often bask in the sun. As it warms up, it starts moving in search of food, or even a mate. As the day becomes hotter, the reptile retreats into the shade to cool down. By shuttling backward and forward, in and out of the shade, the reptile can keep a surprisingly constant internal temperature. A reptile needs to stay warm while it is digesting food – a snake that has eaten, but cannot get to a warm place, may die because the food in its stomach will be too cold to digest. In poor weather, reptiles have low body temperatures; they move slowly and are in danger from predators.

Lizard basking in the heat

KEEPING COOL
In the early morning this agama lizard sits on top of the rock in bright sunlight. After it warms up, it will run around looking for insects to eat. During the hottest part of the day the agama retreats into the shade. If it cools down too much it will creep back onto the rock in the sun. The pattern of warming and cooling down varies with the seasons. For example, during the cool months reptiles are only active at midday, when it is warm, but during the summer months they may go underground at midday to avoid overheating.

Sand lizard

HOT FOOT
When the ground is too hot for its feet, the sand lizard of the Namib Desert "dances," lifting its legs up alternately from the scorching sand. Sometimes, it rests on its belly, lifting all four legs up at the same time. The little ground gecko is also uncomfortable on the hot sand, but it is mainly nocturnal and is usually out when it is cooler.

Ground gecko

TAKING IT EASY
Crocodiles cool down by letting moisture evaporate through their opened mouths, or by simply lying in the cool waters of a muddy stream. American crocodiles lie in burrows or holes when they find the heat too much. On cold nights, crocodiles use the water to stay warm, by sleeping at the bottom of rivers and ponds.

BOILING OVER
Some people turn red with anger as blood rushes to their face, but their blood temperature does not really rise. Committing a deed "in cold blood" – referring to a callous action – is a misinterpretation of the term (pp. 6–7).

TAKING COVER

Like many other desert snakes, the sand viper will do its best to avoid the full heat of the day. It is mainly nocturnal and moves in a "sidewinding" fashion as it hunts for prey (pp. 52–53). It may travel as much as half a mile (1 km) in a single night, searching for its favorite food – small mammals and lizards. If it needs to escape the hot midday sun of the deserts of North Africa and Arabia, it simply sinks itself into the sand.

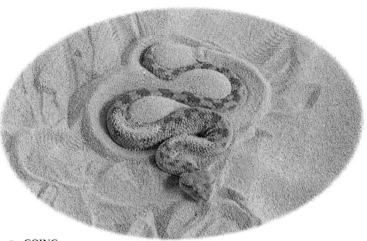

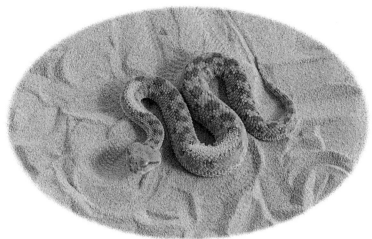

2 GOING...
The snake descends vertically, shuffling and rocking its body. As it goes down, it shovels sand upward and over its back. The scales along the snake help to work the grains of sand along its body.

1 GOING...
A sand viper retreats into the sand, tail first, wriggling as it goes. Its eyes are well protected from irritating grains of sand by the "window" that covers and shields them.

3 GONE!
The sand viper is now almost completely buried. Soon only the top of its head will be visible. Bedding down in the hot desert sand in this way protects it from the scorching sun, and at the same time, makes a perfect hiding place when either enemies or prey are nearby.

Snake leaves very visible marks as it moves in the sand

Uncommon senses

REPTILES HAVE SENSES common to vertebrates – smell, sight, and hearing. They also have other ways of finding out about their surroundings. For example, snakes, and some lizards, "smell" with the help of the tongue and the Jacobson's organ – sensory cells in the roof of the mouth. Some snakes are very sensitive to heat given off by living bodies – which means they can detect warm-blooded prey, even in total darkness. Marine turtles navigate immense distances to their nesting beaches, possibly by using the position of the sun. Or, they may be able to follow magnetic fields caused by electric currents in the water. In some reptiles, certain senses are not very highly developed. For instance, most burrowing reptiles have poor eyesight, and snakes do not hear very well.

ALLIGATOR ROAR
Alligators communicate with one another over vast distances by bellowing. The sound can be very loud, up to 92 decibels at 16 ft (5 m), roughly as loud as the propeller engine of a small airplane!

Swiveling eye is set on a turret

Eyelids can close to tiny peepholes

Pincer-like toes grasp branches

SMALL BUT NOISY
Most geckos make sounds. Certain species produce chirping and clicking noises, usually when mating or defending territory. When distressed, some lizards even produce ultrasounds, which they use to scare off predators. These sounds are detectable by mammals or birds, but are out of the hearing range of the lizards themselves.

BROAD HORIZONS
The chameleon can move its eyes independently and has an extraordinarily wide field of vision. If it sees a fly, it can keep one eye on the fly, while moving toward it. As the chameleon moves, its other eye scans the surroundings, keeping a lookout for possible enemies. When the fly is in range, the chameleon swivels both eyes toward it; at this point the chameleon's eyesight becomes more like the binocular vision of humans. With both eyes firmly fixed on the fly, the chameleon can judge its position more accurately – and take aim.

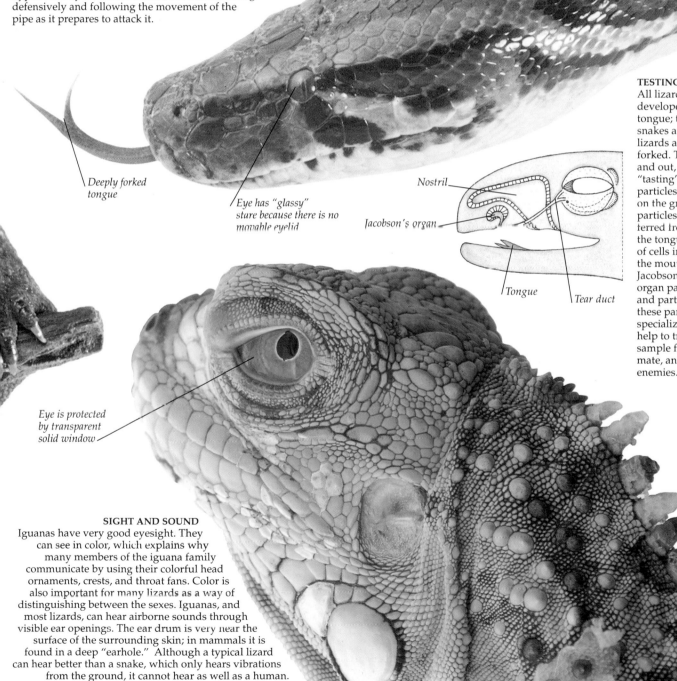

SENSITIVE SOULS
Like all animals, snakes have gradually changed, or evolved, over millions of years. At some point they seem to have gone through a burrowing stage, which affected their senses. Their eyesight and hearing became weaker; their other senses became more acute. Snakes have no external ears. Vibrations from the ground simply move along to the inner ear through skull bones that are joined to the lower jaw. Some snakes have special heat detectors. This Indian python has little heat sensitive pits, or holes, in its lips. These are particularly useful for detecting warm-blooded prey, such as mammals or birds, at night (pp. 42–43).

MUSIC TO ITS EARS
For thousands of years, snakes have been pictured dancing to the music of a pipe played by a charmer. This has led to the mistaken belief that the snakes are somehow hypnotized by the music. In fact, the snake is rising defensively and following the movement of the pipe as it prepares to attack it.

Deeply forked tongue

Eye has "glassy" stare because there is no movable eyelid

Nostril

Jacobson's organ

Tongue

Tear duct

TESTING THE AIR
All lizards have a well-developed, extendable tongue; the tongues of snakes and monitor lizards are deeply forked. They flick in and out, constantly "tasting" chemical particles in the air or on the ground. These particles are transferred from the tip of the tongue to the series of cells in the roof of the mouth called the Jacobson's organ. This organ partly "smells" and partly "tastes" these particles. The specialized tongue can help to trail prey, sample food, find a mate, and detect enemies.

Eye is protected by transparent solid window

SIGHT AND SOUND
Iguanas have very good eyesight. They can see in color, which explains why many members of the iguana family communicate by using their colorful head ornaments, crests, and throat fans. Color is also important for many lizards as a way of distinguishing between the sexes. Iguanas, and most lizards, can hear airborne sounds through visible ear openings. The ear drum is very near the surface of the surrounding skin; in mammals it is found in a deep "earhole." Although a typical lizard can hear better than a snake, which only hears vibrations from the ground, it cannot hear as well as a human.

Dating displays

Reptiles spend most of their time in day-to-day survival, adjusting body heat, searching for food, and escaping from predators. During the mating season, however, they need to be able to attract members of the opposite sex, in order to reproduce. Male lizards often display bright colors and ornate features such as frills and crests to appeal to the females. As in the rest of the animal world, the males may use the same signals that are meant to attract females to warn off male rivals.

DELAYED REACTION
Many snakes can delay egg fertilization, in some cases for months after they have mated. If the old woman of the British nursery rhyme "who had so many children she didn't know what to do" had had the same ability, perhaps her shoe wouldn't have been so crowded.

FLASHY
The male frigate bird attracts his mate in very much the same way the anole lizard does. He keeps his pouch inflated for several hours until she succumbs to his charms.

A COUPLE OF SWELLS
Anole lizards are highly territorial. The males display regularly to one another, inflating their brilliant reddish throat sacs as a sign of aggression. Two lizards of the same size may flaunt this brightly colored flap of skin at one another for hours at a time, though a smaller lizard will retreat immediately if threatened in this way. Anole lizards come from the tropical areas of South and Central America. They are sometimes called "American chameleons," though they are actually iguanas. They blend in well with the green and brown vegetation in which they live. This helps to protect them from their enemies.

SPRING IN THE AIR
Giant tortoises mate in the spring, when the male will often ram the female in the side with his shell to show his interest. The act of mating sometimes takes several hours.

SNAKE CHARMERS
Once a male snake has successfully found a female, he approaches her, then stimulates her into mating by rubbing his chin along her back, while their bodies and tails intertwine. During the mating season, two male snakes will sometimes perform a kind of combat dance, as they vie for a particularly favored female. As they wave their bodies around, often hardly touching each other, they have the opportunity to show who is the bigger and stronger animal. The smaller snake may often be frightened away by this behavior.

MAY THE BEST MAN WIN
At the beginning of the mating season male monitors wrestle, rearing up on their hind legs. The weaker animal finally gives up, usually before it is injured.

Tails intertwined during mating

Throat sac inflated to attract female or as a sign of aggression

Examining eggs

YOUNG REPTILES develop inside an egg, cushioned in a bag of fluid called the amnion. The eggs of most reptiles have a soft and flexible shell, although some have hard shells like birds' eggs. A yolk provides the animal with food, and oxygen and moisture, also necessary for the young reptile's growth and development, are absorbed through the shell. Some lizards and snakes are viviparous, that is, they give birth to fully developed young.

FACT OR FICTION?
In Greek mythology there are many tales about a tribe of warlike women, called the Amazons, who hated men and lived without them. Some all-female lizards, like the little whiptail, can reproduce without mating. This is called parthenogenesis.

Snakes

The eggs of most snakes have a flexible leathery shell. The young snakes hatch by slashing a hole in the shell using a special, sharp egg tooth. Most snakes bury their eggs in a little soil or rotting vegetation. Several vipers, boas, and sea snakes are viviparous.

Ground python egg

Indian python egg

UNDERGROUND COVER
Scarcely recognizable as an egg, this extraordinary-looking object was laid by a ground python, a burrowing snake from West Africa. The egg is large in proportion to the mother. A female of 33 in (85 cm) may lay eggs 5 in (12 cm) in length.

MOTHER LOVE
After laying about 30 of these leathery-shelled eggs, the female Indian python takes unusual care of her precious brood, coiling herself around her eggs. By continuously twitching her muscles (much like shivering) she raises the temperature within the coils several degrees higher than her surroundings.

COMMON AS MUCK
The common African house snake often chooses manure heaps or termite mounds in which to lay its eggs, usually eight or ten at a time.

African house snake egg

Whiptail lizard

Monitor lizard egg

Lizards

Most lizards produce eggs with leathery shells. Lizards are rarely attentive to their eggs once they have been laid. Some skinks, however, return to their nests to brood, raising the temperature of the eggs with their bodies, which have been warmed by the sun.

STUCK ON YOU
The tokay gecko, like many geckos and skinks, lays eggs two at a time. The eggs are soft and sticky at first, but they harden after being exposed to the air. As the eggs dry, they stick to the surface on which they were laid.

Tokay gecko eggs

African chameleon eggs

BURIED ALIVE
Some chameleons give birth to live young; others lay eggs. The African chameleon, which lives in trees, comes down to the ground to lay its clutch of 30 – 40 eggs in a burrow. The chameleon fills in the burrow to protect the eggs; when the young hatch, they have to dig themselves out.

Javan bloodsucker egg

SPINDLE EGGS
The eggs of the tree-dwelling Javan bloodsucker, an agamid lizard, are a most peculiar spindle shape. It is not clear why this is – closely related species have eggs that are more oval in shape.

CUCKOOS IN THE NEST
The Nile monitor lizard likes to lay her eggs in termite mounds. She tears a hole in the side of the mound and then lays 40 – 60 eggs. The heat inside the mound helps to incubate the eggs, which hatch after nine or ten months.

Crocodilians

Caimans and alligators build mounds out of fresh vegetation, soil, and leaf litter to nest their hard-shelled eggs; crocodiles and gavials dig holes for their eggs in exposed beaches and dry, crumbly soil. The female often stays close to the nest to stop would-be thieves from raiding it. All crocodilian eggs have to be kept warm. In fact, the sex of the hatchling is determined by tiny temperature changes during the early stages of incubation.

Dwarf crocodile egg

Alligator egg

WHO'S EATING WHOM?
Humans and crocodiles live side by side along the coast of Papua New Guinea. This shield shows a figure inside the crocodile's belly. The people of Papua New Guinea believed that crocodiles held magical powers.

LENDING A PAW
The female American alligator builds a mound of plant matter and soil, then digs a hole in it to lay 35 – 40 eggs. When the eggs have hatched and the young alligators are ready to leave the nest, they grunt loudly and their mother tears open the nest.

LITTLE MYSTERY
The African dwarf crocodile is basically nocturnal. It lays fewer eggs than most other crocodiles – less than 20 – but they are quite large and are laid directly into a specially constructed mound.

Turtles and tortoises

Tortoises, and some turtles, lay hard-shelled eggs, but the eggshells of marine and some river turtles are soft. Most females make a hole in the ground for their eggs, and they may return to the same spot year after year. As with crocodiles, the sex of baby turtles and tortoises is often determined by the temperature during incubation.

Spur-thighed tortoise egg

Snake-necked turtle egg

Matamata egg

MATAMATA
The eggs of this strange South American turtle look very much like Ping-Pong balls. Like all aquatic turtles, the matamata must leave the water to lay her eggs. These turtles were previously hunted for their meat, but they are now protected by law.

MEDITERRANEAN MATES
The spur-thighed tortoise is found all around the Mediterranean. Up until recently it was exported in large numbers to pet shops in northern European countries. Few of them survived this experience. Importing them is now against the law in many countries.

SNAKE-NECKED TURTLE
The Australian snake-necked turtle leaves the water to lay her eggs in a nest that she digs on dry land. She lays her eggs at night, after rainfall.

Galapagos tortoise egg

GENTLE GIANT
The Galapagos giant tortoise is one of the biggest in the world. It lays its hard-shelled eggs in soil that is exposed to the sun. The eggs sometimes incubate (develop) for 200 days. Unfortunately, many are destroyed by foraging rats and pigs, which were introduced to the islands by humans.

MASS NESTING
Every year some 200,000 Ridley sea turtles come to Orissa, India, to nest along just 3 miles (5 km) of beach. Each female digs a hole in which she lays about 100 eggs, then she returns to the sea.

ADDED PROTECTION
Like birds' eggs, reptilian eggs have a shell which protects the developing young, but also allows it to breathe. The shell is made up of several layers. Here the brittle outer layer has been broken, revealing a flexible inner layer. Under this is the amniotic membrane, which fills with fluid, creating a suitable environment for the developing reptile.

Shell allows embryo to breathe

Embryo

Amnion

Yolk sac

Spitting images

Baby reptiles are born looking like small versions of their parents. Whether they hatch from eggs (pp. 20–21) or are born live, young reptiles are able to feed themselves and can live in much the same environment as they will when they are fully grown. This is fortunate because most reptiles lay their eggs and then move on, leaving the hatchlings to fend for themselves. There are some exceptions. Some lizards and snakes protect their eggs (p. 21), and some watch their young for a period of a few weeks to two years after hatching. A young reptile's eating habits are not the same as its parents'. As the young animal develops, its growing body demands more food. A young crocodile, for example, may be able to survive on insects, but as it grows bigger, it will eat considerably larger prey, including mammals, birds, and fish.

Caiman

LIKE MOTHER LIKE DAUGHTER
This young caiman is born fully formed and able to fend for itself. Like the young alligator, it will stay close to its mother for a few weeks, sometimes using her back as a basking platform. In addition to the mother's protection, unusual in reptiles, the young are able to dive under water for cover at the first sign of danger.

HATCHING
The incubation time – the length of time after an egg is laid and before it hatches – for a snake egg, varies according to the temperature. The warmer it is, the faster the eggs develop, so the parent often chooses to lay them in a place that is both warm and slightly moist. Piles of vegetation produce heat as the plant material rots, so compost heaps are sometimes selected as nesting sites, particularly by snakes living in cooler areas. Once they are laid, snake eggs often swell as they absorb moisture from the environment (pp. 20–21). Often the young snake that emerges is much longer than the egg from which it hatched. This is possible because as the embryo develops, the whole body is coiled into a tight spiral.

1 THE EGG
This is the egg of a rat snake, a large snake common in North America. Its mating season is from April to June. Between June and August the female lays 5–30 soft-shelled, oblong eggs, often choosing rotten wood, leaf litter, or a spot under some rocks as her "nest."

4 MAKING A MOVE
Once it is ready, the snake leaves the egg quickly. It is able to slither along in the normal snake-like way immediately (pp. 52–53). Interestingly, though, if a snake is removed from its egg a little too early, it will writhe about, unable to move properly. However, in every other way it looks normal. It therefore seems likely that the snake only becomes fully coordinated just before hatching.

BIG BABIES
The young of the adder, Britain's only venomous snake, are incredibly large compared with the eggs in which they develop (pp. 20–21).

LOOKS CAN DECEIVE

Most geckos lay their eggs between pieces of bark or stick them to a wall. This sandstone gecko laid her eggs between the crevices of rocks. The eggs have hard shells that protect them from the wind and rain (pp. 20-21). Although many geckos lay their eggs in a common area, they do not take care of their young – in fact, it is unusual that mother and young should be as close to one another as this. The young are independent from birth, but are not sexually mature, that is, able to reproduce, for about 18 months.

Female

Young

THE HAZARDS OF HATCHING
Of all the reptiles, turtles lay the most eggs, but care for them the least. Abandoned to the earth or sand in which its egg was buried, this little hatchling will have to fight alone to survive in a dangerous world.

The young snake checks its surroundings with its tongue

The snake is in no hurry to leave the safety of its shell

2 BREAKING THE SHELL
While it is developing inside the egg, the young rat snake takes nourishment from the yolk. A day or two before hatching, the yolk sac is drawn into the body and the remaining yolk is absorbed into the young snake's intestine. A small scar, much like a belly button, shows the point where the embryo was joined to its food supply. As the young snake develops, a sharp but temporary egg tooth grows from the tip of its upper jaw. The hatchling uses this tooth to pierce the eggshell. The young snake gets its first view of the world through one of the slits it makes.

3 LEAVING THE EGG
Having tested its surroundings by flicking its tongue in and out (pp. 16–17), the hatchling cautiously emerges from its shell. It is in no hurry to leave, and may stay where it is, with only its head poking out, for a day or two. That way, if disturbed, the young snake can always go back inside the egg. Rat snakes are usually ready to leave their eggs 7–15 weeks after being laid.

5 MINOR MIRACLE
It seems amazing that such a long snake could ever have been packed inside such a relatively small egg. The hatchlings may be as much as seven times longer than the egg, or 11–16 in (28–40 cm).

Scale tale

REPTILES HAVE DRY, SCALY SKINS. As in other creatures, the skin forms a barrier between the animal's tissues and the world outside, protecting it from ordinary wear and tear, from drying out, and from damage by predators. The reptiles' scales are thickenings of this outside layer of skin, and are mostly made of a horny substance called keratin, much like fingernails. The outer skin is shed, or molted, from time to time and then renewed by cells in the inner layer. Molting allows room for growth and at the same time replaces worn-out skin. Lizards and snakes have a characteristic molting, or "sloughing," time which varies from species to species. Most lizards shed their skin in large flakes, often over a few days; snakes slough the entire skin at one time.

Old skin is fragile and can break easily

Skin deep

Reptilian skin varies greatly from one species to another. It may be rough, bumpy, or spiny, as on the tails of certain lizards. Or it may form crests on the neck, back, or tail. In most snakes, the belly scales form a series of wide overlapping plates, which help the snakes when moving (pp. 52–53).

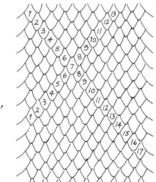

COUNTING THE SCALES
The pattern of scales on different parts of the head and body are valuable in helping specialists to identify reptiles. For example, the number of rows of scales at the midbody line and the number of large belly scales are helpful clues to identifying snakes.

Caiman back

Smooth caiman belly skin

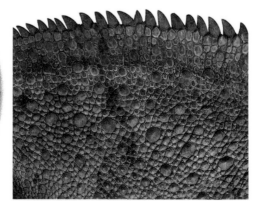

HORNY-SKINNED
The caiman's "armor" is made of rough horny scales, or scutes, along the back and tail. The back scales are strengthened by bony plates.

ON THE CREST
The scales on the back of the chameleon rise to a crest of points along its length.

DIGGERS
The scales of skinks are smooth, so that mud does not cling.

PLATED LIZARD
Like the caiman, this lizard has bony plates under its scales.

New skin is smooth and shiny

RENEWING THE RATTLE
The tail of the rattlesnake is made up of a series of hollow pieces of keratin locked together. Every time the snake sheds its skin, a new segment is added to the rattle. To warn away its enemies, the snake shakes the rattle by vibrating its tail, and the separate pieces knock together to produce the rattle sound. It is a simple, but effective, device.

SLOUGHING
About four times a year, the slowworm sheds its skin in very large pieces. Although it looks like a snake, it is in fact a legless lizard from Europe. Adult lizards molt about once every month when they are most active. Some lizards peel off their old skin in strips with their mouth and swallow the pieces, but the slowworm sheds its old skin more like a snake. The need to molt continues throughout life, because most reptiles never stop growing, though the growth rate is almost undetectable when they are old.

SHARP DRESSING
When a cat sharpens its claws, it is also getting rid of dead tissue. People also shed the dead outer layer of their skin, though they only lose little pieces at a time. Humans need to "shed" their clothes regularly as they grow up, much like a snake needs a new, larger skin. Clothes offer protection from the world around us, as our skin is not as efficient as a reptile's.

ALL IN THE EYE
Several days before a snake is ready to shed its skin, its eyes look cloudy. Its skin appears dull and colorless, it loses its appetite, and may become aggressive. Many snakes also look for water, as they lose a considerable amount of body fluids along with their skins.

NEW SKIN FOR OLD
Snakes are able to crawl out of their old skin, usually leaving it behind in one piece. They can do this because they have no limbs, which might hinder the shedding, and because their outer skin comes off as an all-in-one suit. The sloughing starts along the lips. The snake rubs the side of its head along the ground to turn the skin back; It then crawls out of its skin, turning it inside out as it does so. Often in no more than half an hour the snake emerges, shiny and glistening, in its new colors and scales.

Top

Adult rat snake skin

Young rat snake skin

Underside

Young snakes shed soon after they hatch and then about seven times in their first year

Selection of snakes

ALTHOUGH SNAKES HAVE NO LEGS, eyelids, or eardrums, they can still move quickly and sense their surroundings with special touch and chemical sensors. Snakes are found in many habitats on all continents except Antarctica. Most snakes live on land but some burrow; others live in rivers or the sea, and many climb trees. There are about 2,500 different species. Over 800 of them are poisonous, but only about 250 are considered dangerous to humans.

BOTTOMS UP
When threatened, this harmless, long-nosed snake uses an effective, defensive trick. It hides its head under its coiled body, waves its tail in the air, and shoots blood-stained liquid from its anal opening. It lives in prairies and deserts in the U.S. and Mexico and uses its pointed snout to burrow.

BACK BITER
This mildly venomous, rear-fanged Madagascan hognose snake rarely bites people. It feeds on small mammals and amphibians, but if it is threatened, it will flatten its neck (like a cobra) and hiss loudly. It shelters in burrows in grassland areas on the island of Madagascar, and grows up to 5 ft (152 cm) long.

NIGHT-TIME PROWLER
Another snake harmless to people is the California mountain kingsnake. It is also one of the most colorful snakes found in North America. When the weather is warm, this snake rests during the day and hunts at night for lizards, other snakes, and young birds. It is 40 in (102 cm) long and is found from northern California to southern Washington State.

CHECKMATE
This non-poisonous snake from the eastern U.S. is called the corn snake because the checked markings on its underside look like the pattern of kernals on an ear of corn. The longest on record measured 6 ft (183 cm).

SHRINKING VIOLET
This shy, gray-banded kingsnake is rarely seen in the wild. Despite its secretive habits, this harmless snake is a popular pet and has bred successfully in captivity. It is 4 ft (121 cm) when fully grown, and lives on a diet of lizards.

STONY LOOK
Medusa was a terrifying mythical being. Her head was covered with writhing snakes, and anyone unlucky enough to glance at her would instantly turn to stone.

BEGONE!

Legend has it that Ireland has no snakes because St. Patrick banished them to rid the country of evil.

IN THE BEGINNING

Snakes have not been very popular since the time of the Garden of Eden, when the devil, in the form of a serpent, tempted Eve with the forbidden fruit. This painting of that scene, by Albrecht Dürer, was painted in 1504.

STOCK-STILL

The vine snake from Southeast Asia spends hours hanging in a tree, motionless. Because it is bright green and very slender, it is well hidden. Its eyes face forward, giving it binocular vision. As a result, it is good at judging distances, especially when lunging at passing lizards.

DOUBLE BLUFF

This harmless Sinaloan milk snake, looks very like the highly venomous coral snake, which probably deters quite a few predators from trying to make a meal of the snake. Milk snakes are so-called because of a mistaken belief that they steal milk from cows.

THE PITS

The copperhead is a North American member of the pit viper family. Like its relatives the rattlesnakes, the copperhead can inflict a nasty bite, its venom entering the victim's bloodstream, causing internal bleeding. However, people rarely die from copperhead bites. These snakes grow to about 3 ft (91 cm).

Eye facing forward

HIGH FLIER

The flying snake is an energetic, fast-moving tree snake from southern Asia. It is active by day and hangs high up in the trees of thick forests hunting for lizards and the occasional frog. It jumps from branch to branch and even glides through the air to lower levels. When it wants to slow down, it flattens its body to increase air resistance.

Loads of lizards

MEEK AND MILD
In spite of its fierce appearance, the spiky moloch is harmless. It lives almost exclusively on ants. In addition to giving predators a prickly mouthful, the moloch's spikes have another use: dew condenses on them and runs into the lizard's mouth. In this way, the lizard can live for weeks without drinking.

THERE ARE OVER 3,000 SPECIES OF LIZARD. They form the most successful of all the reptilian groups, having evolved many different life-styles. Although most of them live on the ground, many live in trees, some burrow, and still more live in water. Some lizards have no limbs and are very snake-like. Others can parachute or fly. Geckos, iguanas, chameleons, skinks, and monitors are just a few of the lizards alive today.

PUNK IS ALIVE
The common iguana's crest, running like the teeth of a comb down the center of the lizard's back, makes it easy to spot. These lizards are often seen basking in trees.

BLUE MOVER
The blue-tongued skink is so-called because of its blue tongue, which it constantly flicks in and out. This skink gives birth to live young. And despite its clumsy appearance it can move fast when necessary.

KOMODO KING
The Komodo dragon, a monitor lizard, is the largest living lizard in the world. One captured specimen was 10 ft 2 in (3.10 m) in length and weighed a staggering 365 lb (165.6 kg). The dragon is found only on a few Indonesian islands.

ARMOR-PLATED
Plated lizards have tough, bony plates underlying their scales. These lizards normally have long tails but this one has clearly had a narrow escape and its tail has not yet regrown fully (pp. 24–25).

FLAT AS A PANCAKE
This African lizard, like many of its family, has a flat body and thick protective scales, and it can slip easily into cracks in boulders. When threatened by a predator, it can jam itself into a crevice where it inflates its body, so that it is very difficult to pry out.

COLOR CONSCIOUS
Chameleons generally lead calm lives, which is fortunate, as aside from their ability to change color, they have few defenses against enemies. The male Jackson's chameleon is better off than most – his prehistoric-looking, three-pronged horns probably frighten away many foes.

BLINKING GECKOS
Leopard geckos are unusual in that they have movable eyelids. Most geckos, like snakes, cannot blink, but have a fixed, transparent window protecting their eyes. Their toes end in tiny pads with many hairlike projections, which can cling to smooth surfaces.

TREE CREEPER
The glossy-skinned, emerald tree skink rarely ventures onto the ground, and spends most of its life scuttling amid the branches of trees in Indonesia.

Emerald tree skink

A TOE-TO-TAIL TALE
Chameleons have truly remarkable toes, specialized for life in trees. The toes are arranged so that the feet are able to clasp branches securely. The tail offers extra support, twisting and twining itself around any handy branch. This Madagascan chameleon, like many others, also boasts a strange, sticky-tipped tongue which it can shoot out farther than the length of its body, guaranteeing it a good diet of insects and other small invertebrates.

GOOD INFLUENCE
In Chinese art, the common lizard has evolved into a magnificent dragon. The dragon in Chinese folklore is the symbol of rebirth and fertility. Because it is thought to be a gentle creature spreading happiness, it plays a large part in the famous street festivals of many Chinese communities.

Strong tail aids posture and balance

EYED LIZARD
The eyed or ocellated lizard is only found in Europe and North Africa. It is one of Europe's largest lizards, sometimes growing to a length of 2 ft 7 in (80 cm). This shy lizard is really a ground dweller but can climb well.

Turtles and tortoises

CHELONIANS, OR REPTILES WITH SHELLS, are found in warm or hot climates in most parts of the world. There are between 250 and 300 species. The shell protects the reptile from knocks and bumps, poor weather conditions, and predators. It is also good camouflage. Chelonians live in salt water, fresh water, and on land. Marine chelonians are called turtles and the rest are tortoises, but sometimes pond and river dwellers are known as terrapins. All chelonians lay eggs on land in a variety of different habitats. Some lay in sand, some in leaf litter, and some in the burrows of other animals. The number of eggs laid varies with the body size of the mother. The smaller species lay one to four eggs per clutch, whereas some large sea turtles regularly lay over 100 eggs at a time.

TURTLE GOD
In Brahmin mythology, after one of the great floods, the god Vishnu returned to earth as the turtle Kurma. He came to help rescue the world.

GALAPAGOS GIANTS
Charles Darwin wrote about the Galapagos Islands of the Pacific Ocean in 1835. He found the giant tortoises had adapted to life on their own island. There are two main groups: the saddlebacks, which reach up to tall vegetation for their food, and the domeshells, which graze on the ground.

LONESOME GEORGE
On the island of Santa Cruz in the Galapagos Islands, a giant tortoise, nearly 3 ft (1 m) in length, lives alone. He appears to be the last remaining giant tortoise from neighboring Pinta Island. Many attempts have been made to find a female from the same island, but without success. It seems George will live and die alone.

The carapace covers the back

HALF AND HALF
Pond terrapins are mainly vegetarian and spend most of their time in water, though they do come onto land to bask. The lungs of some of the pond terrapins of southern Asia are enclosed in bony boxes formed by the inner walls of the shell. This box protects the lungs from increased pressure when the animals dive to great depths. The European pond terrapin is found throughout Europe, western Asia, and northwest Africa. It is a shy creature and dives into the water when approached.

The plastron covers the belly

The shell is made up of 59 to 61 bones and is in two parts, the plastron and the carapace

RED EARS
Red-eared terrapins got their name because of the broad, red stripe that runs along the side of the head. Because they are gentle and attractive creatures they are very popular as pets. Unfortunately, they seldom reach maturity in captivity because they do not receive the vitamins and minerals they need. They live in ponds and rivers in the U.S., but frequently climb out of the water to bask, often on logs, where they may pile up several deep.

The red or yellow "ear marking" makes this turtle instantly recognizable

The plastron and carapace are joined on each side by a girdle bone

LETHAL SOFTY
The shell of soft-shelled turtles has no horny plates and feels like leather. In Africa, Asia, Indonesia, and North America they are usually found buried in mud in rivers and ponds, though like many other turtles they enjoy basking in the sun. They are able to breathe while in the water by stretching their long necks to the surface and taking a breath through the snorkel-like nose. They hide from enemies but are fierce and effective hunters and can strike at lightning speed.

RECORD REPTILE
The leatherback is the largest of all living turtles, and according to some records, it is also the heaviest. In 1988 this enormous leatherback drowned when it became entangled in fishermen's line. It was washed up in Harlech Bay in Wales. It weighed 2,016 lb (752 kg), and is the biggest turtle ever recorded. These turtles breed in the Caribbean, then follow jellyfish, their main food, across the Atlantic.

Hawksbill turtle shell

Large scales, called scutes, cover the bone of the shell

Starred tortoise shell

Radiated tortoise shell

SHELLS
Different life-styles lead to alterations in shell structure. Tortoises usually have high-domed or knobby shells as protection against a predator's strong jaws. Turtles tend to have flatter shells, which are streamlined for easy movement through the water. The soft-shelled turtles have the flattest shells, which allow them to hide easily beneath sand and mud.

Turtle tank

IN FOLKLORE, THE ALLIGATOR SNAPPING TURTLE was thought to be a cross between a common turtle and an alligator. It is well-named because it is ferocious both in appearance and in its habits. Its powerful knifelike jaws can do considerable damage to a person's fingers and toes. It spends nearly all its time in water. When fishing for prey, the animal lies motionless on the river bed, its mouth wide open. It will eat practically anything that it can catch, including snails and clams and even other turtles. Any object too large to swallow in one piece is simply chopped in half by the jaws. It is one of the largest freshwater turtles in the world and can grow to 26 in (66 cm) and weigh up to 200 lb (91 kg).

Wormlike appendage

Sharp jaws used to cut prey

WIGGLY WORM
One of the most remarkable features of the alligator snapper is the wormlike appendage on the end of its tongue. This "worm" fills with blood, which colors it red; it then resembles an earthworm on a fishing hook. It has a wide "tail" end and a narrow "head" end. When hungry, the turtle lies very still on the bottom of the river, opens its mouth, and wiggles the "worm." Unwary prey pass by, dive in after the bait, and the jaws of the turtle snap shut.

Turtle rises on its forelegs when faced with an aggressor

*Bumpy, ridged
shell provides
both protection
and camouflage*

*Very powerful forelegs
often used to hold prey*

UNSAFE TO BATHE
The alligator snapper looks
very much like a stone, especially when its ridged shell is
covered with algae. It relies on
this superb camouflage to trap
its prey. Careless bathers in this
river could have their toes
severely damaged by the
blade-like jaws.

The crocodile clan

CROCODILES, along with their relatives the alligators, caimans, and gavials, are ancient animals. They belong to the same group of creatures that included the dinosaurs and the ancestors of the birds. The crocodile family spends a lot of time basking in the sun or lying in water. But when necessary they can move tremendously fast, attacking with immense power and precision. Despite their ferocity, crocodile parents are more attentive to their young than any other group of living reptiles. The same smiling jaws that can kill an animal as huge as a wildebeest can carry and protect babies only inches long.

CROCODILE GOD
Sobek, the crocodile god of ancient Egypt, gradually evolved from a minor protective god into one of the most important of all the Egyptian deities. No one knows whether he became a god because he was so feared.

Gavial skull
(top view)

EGYPTIAN MUMMIES
In ancient Egypt many animals, including the crocodile, were sacred. In some of the temples, crocodiles were looked after in special pools, draped with pendants of gold and precious stones. When they died they were embalmed, or mummified.

A STITCH IN TIME
Mary Queen of Scots was held as a prisoner by Queen Elizabeth I from 1569 to 1584. She and her jailer set to work embroidering this massive wall hanging. The crocodile is just one of the many animal hangings they produced. Presumably the work had a calming effect on Mary as she awaited her execution.

GAVIAL
The gavial, strangest of all the crocodiles, has a long narrow snout with small, piercing teeth. As the snout sweeps through the water, the interlocking and outwardly pointing teeth grasp slippery fish. The adult male wards off rivals with a loud buzz made through the knob, or ghara, on its nose. The noise, produced as the gavial breathes out, is useful because the animal's jaws are not particularly powerful.

Gavial skull
(side view)

Caiman

Caiman skull
(side view)

Caiman skull
(top view)

CAIMAN

Caimans are members of the alligator family. Their snouts are rather short and broad, and, as with alligators, the teeth on the lower jaw are largely invisible when the mouth is closed. Young caimans eat mainly insects, but as they grow, their diet grows too, to include water snails, fish, mammals, and birds. One species of broad-snouted caiman is particularly adaptable and has been seen in cattle ponds and in heavily polluted rivers near large cities.

Crocodile skull
(side view)

Prominent tooth

Eye sockets

Crocodile skull
(top view)

CROCODILE

In crocodiles some of the teeth on the lower jaw stick out above the upper jaw when the mouth is shut. They are perfect for gripping and puncturing, but are not so good at slicing and chewing. When a crocodile is eating an animal as large as a buffalo, it will seize part of the carcass in its jaws, and roll over and over until a chunk is torn away.

Alligator skull
(side view)

Lower jaw openings

ALLIGATOR

The American alligator can use its jaws with surprising delicacy. The female, for example, sometimes helps her eggs hatch by lifting them into her mouth, where she gently cracks them open by rolling them against the roof of her mouth with her tongue. The alligator is a massive creature, reaching up to 20 ft (6 m) in length.

Alligator skull
(top view)

External nostrils

The living fossil

THE TUATARA IS CALLED A "LIVING FOSSIL" because it is the sole survivor of an order of reptiles that is otherwise extinct. In fact, it is remarkable that the tuatara has survived, and no one really knows why, since its closest relatives died out millions of years ago. Today, tuataras live on a few small islands off the coast of New Zealand, where they are active at night. They inhabit burrows that are also often occupied by sea birds (pp. 60–61). Although the tuatara looks like a lizard, it differs from lizards in a number of ways. Tuataras have a low metabolic rate (the rate at which food is converted into energy) and are able to function well in much colder temperatures than other reptiles. They also have an extremely slow growth rate and are sometimes still growing at 50–60 years of age.

Male

Female

KITH OR KIN?
These are the fossilized remains of *Homoeosaurus*, a tuatara-like animal that lived about 140 million years ago in what is now Europe. "Sphenodontida," the group that contains the tuatara and its fossil relatives, were very widespread and successful animals at that time. It seems likely that the sphenodontids separated from early lizards some 200 million years ago.

Short, strong legs suitable for excavating burrows

36

Tuatara, a word meaning "peaks on the back," refers to the crest that runs down the back and tail

RESURRECTION

Another true living fossil is the coelacanth, which means "hollow spine." It was the name given to a group of fish that lived from 300 to 90 million years ago. After that time they were thought to be extinct and were known only as fossils. However, in 1938, a live coelacanth was caught off the coast of South Africa, and there were hopes that other coelacanths might live in the region. But it was not until 14 years later that the coelacanth "home" was discovered in deep waters off the coast of the Comoro Islands, northwest of Madagascar in the Indian Ocean.

GROWING OLD TOGETHER

Male tuataras grow to a length of about 2 ft (61 cm); females are slightly shorter. They reach sexual maturity at about 20 years of age and can possibly live to more than 120. They have no external ear openings and the male has no external sexual organ. After mating, the female stores the sperm for 10–12 months, after which she lays 5–15 eggs in a shallow burrow. The eggs do not hatch for another 15 months, the longest incubation period of any reptile, and the young are self-sufficient immediately after birth.

A third "eye," sensitive to light, is visible in the young animal. The skin thickens over this organ in the adult. It may regulate the "biological clock" of the tuatara and also possibly acts as a thermostat

Teeth are part of the jawbone which has serrated (notched) edges

Bony arches

SKULL STRUCTURE

The tuatara's skull differs from that of lizards in that two bony arches frame the back, more like a crocodilian's. In most lizards, the lower arch is missing; in snakes and many burrowing lizards both arches have gone.

ODD MEN OUT

Although the duck-billed platypus and the spiny echidna are not strictly "living fossils," they are certainly primitive and very unusual mammals. The platypus has the bill of a duck and the tail of a beaver; the spiny anteater bears a strong resemblance to a hedgehog. Like reptiles, both these mammals are egg-layers.

Duck-billed platypus

Echidna (spiny anteater)

A bite to eat

MOST REPTILES ARE MEAT-EATERS, or carnivores. Crocodiles and snakes are all carnivores and have perfected methods of eating their food. Some snakes have specialized diets, such as only birds' eggs (pp. 44–45) or only fish eggs (eaten by some sea snakes). Many lizards are also predators, feeding on insects, mammals, birds, and other reptiles. The Komodo dragon has serrated (notched) teeth much like a shark's, which it uses to cut chunks of flesh from prey as big as water buffalos. Some lizards, however, are mostly vegetarian, including large iguanas, some of the bigger skinks, and a few agamids. Tortoises eat a variety of plants, but even they occasionally eat meat. Terrapins often eat worms, snails, fish, and other small animals. Sea turtles generally feed on jelly-fish, crabs, mollusks, and fish, but they also eat plants. In fact, the green turtle eats little besides sea grass.

SLOW BUT SURE
Very few tortoises or turtles have the speed or agility to catch fast-moving prey. As a result, most feed on vegetation or on slow-moving animals, such as mollusks, worms, and insect larvae. They all make the most of food that is nearby. The spur-thighed tortoise eats fleshy plants but enjoys the occasional piece of dead animal it finds.

HOOK MEETS HIS END
In J. M. Barrie's *Peter Pan*, Hook is haunted by the crocodile that has already eaten his hand – and is looking for more! Usually warned of its presence by a clock that ticks in the creature's stomach, Hook is finally tricked.

CROCODILE LARDER
Nile crocodiles occasionally share the carcass of a large animal such as a wildebeest or a buffalo. Crocodile stomachs are only the size of a basketball, so crocodiles cannot eat a big animal all at once. Prey is often left in one spot to be finished off later. This has led to the mistaken belief that crocodiles like to eat rotten meat, hiding a freshly killed animal until it is "high," or spoiled. In fact, they prefer fresh meat.

Armlets

Pieces of turtle shell

Stones

Bangle

Porcupine quills

STOMACH STORE
Crocodiles often devour hard, heavy objects, such as stones and pieces of metal, possibly to help them digest their food. One can only hope that no one was wearing the bangle when it was swallowed!

Shed tooth   Tooth in use

Developing tooth

DEVELOPING TEETH
Mammals grow only two sets of teeth – baby, or "milk" teeth, and then eventually a set of adult teeth. Crocodiles shed their teeth throughout their lives, with new ones constantly replacing old ones. The developing teeth grow up through the holes of those already in use.

Eyed lizards are primarily ground-dwellers, but are also excellent climbers. Crickets and grasshoppers are their favorite food

CRISPY CRICKET

After a rapid chase, the eyed lizard grabs a cricket with its jaws and shakes its victim violently to stun it. The lizard passes the cricket to the back of its mouth, its jaws moving over the prey in a succession of snapping movements. The lizard's teeth grip and release the cricket as the jaws are raised and lowered. It is important that the lizard moves fast – the cricket may not yet be totally stunned and will not waste an opportunity to try to escape. The majority of lizards are insect-eaters and in some areas are helpful in keeping insect populations down.

SHARPSHOOTERS

Chameleons have tongues as long as their bodies and tails and have been described as the sharpshooters of the lizard world. The tongue is hollow and unforked and has a large, sticky tip. It is shot from the mouth at lightning speed and with tremendous accuracy by a contracting muscle. A second set of muscles draws the tongue back into the mouth, where it is kept bunched up until it is needed again.

A tight squeeze

ALL SNAKES EAT MEAT, and they have had to develop many different ways of killing their food. Many snakes kill their prey with venom (pp. 42–43), but boas and pythons kill by squeezing, or constricting, their prey. Constrictors, which eat mainly mammals, do not crush their victims as many people think. The snake coils its body around its struggling victim, making it harder and harder for the prey to breathe, until it finally suffocates. The snake applies just enough pressure to match the breathing movements of its prey. Any mammal, from a mouse to a deer, may become a snake's victim, depending on the size of the snake. In fact, giant snakes can swallow surprisingly big animals. An anaconda over 25 ft (8 m) long can eat a caiman nearly 6 ft (2 m) long, though it may take more than a week to digest.

TINTIN TO THE RESCUE!
There are a few Asian and African records of humans who have been killed and eaten by some of the larger species of pythons. In one of the well-known *Tintin* books, Zorrino the guide has a lucky escape (contrary to appearances here), saved just in time by his friend Tintin.

DANGEROUS ACT
Circus act performers who dance with constrictors are taking a great risk. This drawing is of a dancer who was nearly suffocated by a python – and was rescued only seconds before certain death.

2 DEADLY EMBRACE
The constricting snake reacts to every minute movement of the rat, tightening its grip all the time. It responds to even the smallest vibrations produced by the rat's beating heart, and the snake will not release its hold until the beating finally stops. Death comes fairly quickly and bones are rarely broken. The snake shifts the rat into a good position so that it can be swallowed head first. That way it slips down the throat quite easily.

3 BIG MOUTH
The snake's mouth is very flexible. Each bone can move individually – up and down, back and forth, and from side to side – while the backward-pointing teeth grip tightly. As the powerful jaws move over the head of the rat, it looks as though the snake is "walking over" its food.

4 SAFETY FIRST
It may take the snake an hour or more to swallow some of its larger victims. The prey is drawn in by the snake's trunk muscles. The snake then forms a sharp curve in its neck behind the prey and pushes it down into the stomach. If, however, the snake is frightened while it is eating, it can regurgitate (spit out) its meal in order to escape swiftly.

Body can expand to allow for large prey

5 TIGHT FIT
Now, most of the rat has disappeared. The flexible ligament, much like an elastic muscle that connects the two halves of the snake's lower jaw, allows the snake to open its mouth very wide. As the lower jaws are forced apart, the muscle between them stretches to the shape of the prey.

DINNER TIME
A snake can usually afford to ignore a prey that could put up a dangerous fight. After an enormous feast – for example, an entire leopard – the snake may not eat again for as much as a year.

1 FANGS OF DEATH
When a hungry boa constrictor attacks its prey, it looks for an end where it can start swallowing – usually the head end. If the victim is wriggly and fat, like this rat, the snake will strike with its long front teeth. Having secured the rat in its jaws, the snake starts to coil around it.

Jaw closed

Jaw open

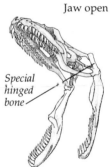

Special hinged bone

OPEN WIDE
The jaws of a snake are very flexible, so prey can be swallowed headfirst and whole, even when the victim's body is wider than the snake's. A special bone, linking the lower jaw to the skull, works like a double-jointed hinge. The lower jaw can be stretched sideways, because the two halves are connected at the chin by a flexible ligament that works like an elastic muscle.

SNAKE EATS SNAKE
When a California king snake meets a rattlesnake, it grips the rattler with its jaws just behind the head. Then the king snake loops its body around the victim, squeezing until the rattler suffocates.

WILD CAT STRIKE
In Kenya, a Thompson's gazelle falls victim to a cheetah. The massive jaws of the cat clamp on to the throat of the struggling prey, possibly causing it to suffocate. But no one really knows whether the gazelle dies by suffocation – in the same way as a boa's prey – or whether it is finished off by the sharp, pointed teeth and powerful claws of the cheetah.

6 THE END OF THE ROAD
At this point the snake could face breathing difficulties, but it overcomes the problem by pushing its windpipe forward towards the front of its mouth using it as a built-in "snorkel".

Name your poison

POISONOUS SNAKES ARE FOUND in many parts of the world in most habitats, but the most poisonous species tend to be concentrated in tropical areas. A snake injects poison, or venom, into its prey, using specially adapted teeth or fangs. In the most dangerous venomous snakes, such as vipers, cobras, and sea snakes, the fangs are found at the front of the upper jaw, but in other snakes they are sometimes at the back. The venom itself is a complicated "cocktail" that affects the prey's nervous system, tissues, or blood – or all three. Its main purpose is to subdue the prey so that the snake can then kill it, but the snake also uses venom to defend itself. However, most snakes will try to avoid a fight, escaping when possible.

Cheek muscles contract, forcing venom out

CRUEL TO BE KIND
In many parts of the world, people still milk snakes for their venom, as venom is used to produce serum (fluid used in medicines to prevent the action of poison) against snake bites. The snake is held by the back of the head and made to bite through tissue covering the top of a small container. It is then forced to eject the venom by gentle pressure on the venom sac in the cheeks. In time, the animal produces more venom.

RATTLESNAKE
Rattlesnakes are extremely venomous snakes. They are sometimes known as pit vipers because they have a remarkably keen heat-sensitive pit between their nostrils and eyes that enables them to locate prey at night. Even in total darkness, they can detect and strike accurately at objects only a fraction of a degree warmer than their surroundings. A rattlesnake's age cannot be determined by the number of rattles on its tail, as some people believe. In fact, the snake may shed its skin and add a new rattle two or three times a year.

Sea snake

Gila monster

OTHER POISONERS
The sea snake is the most venomous snake in the world. It can swim extremely fast and stay under water for up to five hours. There are two species of poisonous lizard – the Gila monster and the Mexican beaded lizard. Both are found in the southwestern U.S. and in parts of Mexico. Their venom comes from saliva glands in the lower jaw, and the lizards chew it into the victim.

Venom passes through tube

Hole in the tip of the fang

Venom sac

FANG FACTS
A rattlesnake's fangs lay against the roof of the mouth until needed, then the upper jaw bone rotates, bringing the fangs forward for biting. Snakes use one pair at a time; one or more spare pairs are arranged in formation behind them.

SOLO SHREW
The short-tailed shrew is the only mammal with a venomous bite. It has glands in its mouth that produce a nerve poison. When this little creature bites its prey, usually smaller mammals, the venom in the saliva enters the wound and is powerful enough to kill in seconds.

STAR PERFORMERS

Snakes have appeared in literature for hundreds of years. In Shakespeare's *Antony and Cleopatra*, Cleopatra commited suicide using an asp, a type of cobra commonly found in Egypt and East Africa. The asp's bite is deadly from the moment the snake leaves the shell. Snakes have also starred in films, such as *True Grit*. Here, John Wayne examines Kim Darby's hand after she has been bitten.

Antony and Cleopatra

SNAKE STONES

Snake stones were once thought to cure snakebites. They were often made of burned bone, chalk, horn, or other absorbent materials, which were believed to "absorb" the venom from a bite when pressed against it.

Special scales make up rattle

Hollow segments which lock together

Rattle

Rapid vibration produces a sizzling sound

Egg-eating snakes

SOME SNAKES EAT NOTHING but eggs and have become specially adapted for the task. Small eggs, especially the soft-shelled ones laid by lizards and some snakes, are easy to eat, as they can be quickly slit open by the snake's teeth. Larger, hard-shelled eggs, such as those laid by birds, need special treatment. True egg-eating snakes eat only birds' eggs, which they swallow whole. These snakes have few teeth, instead they have toothlike spines on the backbone that crack open the egg as it passes down through the snake's throat.

Diet of eggs

One problem with an egg diet is that food is not always available. In some parts of the world, birds only lay their eggs at certain times of the year, and so a snake may have to go a long time without food. Fortunately, egg-eating snakes can bring up, or regurgitate, eggshell. This means that no space is wasted in the snake's stomach, and it can eat as many eggs as it finds. It also means the snake does not waste vital energy digesting the shell.

2 SWALLOW HARD
The egg is passing down the snake's throat. The skin on the side of the neck is very elastic. At this stage the egg is still unbroken.

Head arches down, pushing egg against bony inner spines to puncture shell

Finely interlinked scales, which separate as skin stretches

3 SPINY BONES
The passage of the egg has now been stopped by the toothlike spines on the underside of the neck bones.

A valve at the entrance to the stomach accepts yolks and liquids, but rejects pieces of shell

The "bulge" is noticeably smaller

4 GOING DOWN...
Once the egg has been punctured, the muscles of the snake's body work in waves to squeeze out the contents, which then continue on to the stomach. The snake now bends its body into S-shaped curves, forcing the collapsed shell back toward the mouth.

5 AND UP IT COMES...
It may take from five minutes to an hour for the egg to be completely swallowed, depending on its size. Finally, the snake gapes widely and the compacted cigar-shaped shell is brought up. The fragments of shell are still held together by the sticky egg membranes.

The jagged edges of the shell pieces are stuck together. All the contents of the egg have been drained

Regurgitated shell

1 TOO GREEDY?

An African egg-eater is about to swallow an egg. It looks impossible – the egg is twice the width of the snake's body. The snake has a lightly built skull and its mouth is lined with sticky ridges.

Mouth ridges grip the egg as it passes toward the snake's throat

Because of its shape, an egg is remarkably resistant to crushing before it is pierced by the snake's bony spines

STOP! THIEF!

Monitor lizards, which include some of the giants of the reptilian world, are well-known for their greed. They feed on live animals and on the carcasses of dead animals. A nest of eggs is not safe with these lizards around.

Survival

REPTILES USE A VARIETY OF METHODS to frighten away their enemies. Some can camouflage themselves (pp. 48–49) to avoid being seen in the first place. Others may scare predators by inflating themselves with air, then blowing it out with a loud hiss. Several lizards and some snakes try to protect their vulnerable head and trunk by sacrificing their tail. Some horned lizards swell up in defense, and at the same time squirt blood from tiny blood vessels, or capillaries, in the eyes. It is possible that the blood irritates other animals' eyes. The armadillo lizard from South Africa protects its soft-skinned belly by coiling itself up into a tight ball. Although it cannot escape by rolling away in this position, its thick, spiny scales running the length of its head, back, and tail, create an effective shield.

ON GUARD

One of the most spectacular displays of any reptile is that of the Australian frilled lizard. The "frill" is a large flap of loose skin that is attached to the neck and is normally kept folded flat. When startled by a predator, the lizard erects this rufflelike collar, so that it is often more than four times the width of its body. If challenged, the lizard will also start to bob its head, lash its tail, and wave its legs around. Though most lizards under attack will normally try to escape, the frilled lizard meets danger head on if predators get too close for comfort.

Gaping mouth expands the neck frill. The wider the mouth is opened, the more erect the frill becomes

WHAT A STINKER

The skunk is a mammal that is well-known for the foul smell it produces when frightened or threatened. The stinkpot is a North American turtle that is just as evil-smelling as its name suggests. The smell is produced by a pair of glands in the soft skin of the turtle's thighs when it is frightened. It is also aggressive so it is unlikely to be attacked by too many predators.

Frill fully erected to scare aggressors

Tail is lashed back and forth

Stinkpot

Skunk

Extended claws and flexed feet provide balance

SURVIVAL KIT

If people are to survive in adverse conditions, they have to use special clothes and equipment. Though reptiles cannot survive extreme temperatures, they can adapt to changing weather conditions within their own environment.

THE TALE OF A TAIL

When grabbed by the tail, most lizards will shed it. Though a dramatic method of defense, loss of a tail is better than certain death. Several lizards waggle their tail when first attacked and this helps to confuse the attacking animal. The vertebrae, or small backbones, along the tail have special cracks marking the spots where it can break off. When the tail is grasped, the muscles, which are also arranged so that they will separate neatly, contract. This causes one of the vertebrae to break off.

Fracture points along the tail

1 BREAKING FREE

This tree skink has lost part of its tail while breaking free from a predator. The shed part of the tail often twitches for several minutes after it has been severed, confusing the enemy for long enough for the lizard to escape.

Tail has been recently shed

Although the new tail looks the same on the outside, it has a simple tube of cartilage instead of vertebrae on the inside

2 GROWING STRONGER

In two months the tail has grown back noticeably. Losing it was costly, however. The lizard may have been storing food in it for a time when there might be little or none around, such as in winter or during a dry season. Some species are also known to live longer when they have a complete tail.

3 NEW FOR OLD

After eight months the tail has grown almost to its original full length. If necessary, the tail can be broken off again, but it will only be able to break in the old part, where there are still vertebrae and "cracking points."

Growing a new tail uses up a lot of energy that could have been put to better use

PLAYING DEAD

When all else fails, some snakes will pretend to be dead. When this European grass snake first meets an enemy it puffs and hisses loudly. If this does not work, the snake will roll over onto its back, wriggle (as though in the last stages of death), and then lie still, with its mouth wide open and its tongue hanging out. Although pretending to be dead may fool some animals, if the snake is turned over, it will roll on its back again, giving the game away!

Blending in

MANY REPTILES ARE ABLE TO CHANGE their appearance in order to make themselves hard to see against their natural background. This ability, known as camouflage, is used to avoid being spotted by enemies; it is also used to help the reptile ambush unsuspecting prey. Some reptiles are naturally camouflaged, and their skin color matches their background perfectly. In other reptiles, the pattern on the skin helps to break up the outline of the body. In a few, it is the shape of the animal that camouflages it. For example, the fleshy side fringes and leaf-shaped tail of a tree-living gecko, helps it blend almost perfectly with the bark and lichen of the tree trunks it clings to.

COLOR CONSCIOUS
Lizards, especially chameleons, are the true masters of camouflage. Many can make the color of their skin lighter or darker as needed. Although these changes take place so that the chameleon can match its background, many other things influence the color change. Light level, temperature, and the mood of the lizard (for example if it is frightened) can all affect the color it takes on.

The chameleon's skin has several layers of color cells. Beneath these are the melanophores, cells with tentacle-like arms that extend through the other layers.

The color change is caused by the melanophores moving a dark brown pigment in and out of the upper layers of the skin.

LEAF GREEN
Hard to spot against the palm trees on which they are commonly found, these little tree skinks live in the forests of Indonesia, the Philippines, and the Solomon Islands. The bright green and mottled brown of their bodies, make them almost invisible. Green is understandably a popular color among tree-living reptiles active in the day.

FLOWER POWER
Do not be fooled by this little head. Beneath the leafy canopy is the large body of the Murray River turtle from eastern Australia. It is a powerful swimmer and is mainly carnivorous, though it will eat a few plants.

DOUBLE TROUBLE

Lying still in the leaf litter of the forests of tropical Africa, these gaboon vipers are nearly invisible in the dappled light and shade, as they wait for rodents, frogs, and birds. Yet when one of the snakes is removed from its natural background, its vivid markings become strikingly obvious. Many people have compared the colorful geometrical skin patterns to those on oriental carpets. Although unaggressive and unlikely to attack, this snake's bite would be dangerously venomous to anyone unfortunate enough to tread on one! In fact, the fangs of the gaboon viper are the longest of any snake, up to 2 in (50 mm) in a 6 ft (1.8 m) specimen

Gaboon viper

HIDDEN DEPTHS

Luckily for this black caiman, it is often mistaken for rocks as it lies in the muddy waters. Its ability to lie unseen helps it when it is looking for food. It is hunted for its skin and so is constantly threatened.

Lots of legs

THE LEGS AND FEET of a reptile accurately reflect the animal's life-style. They are usually specifically adapted to the habitat in which the reptile lives. Desert lizards, for example, often have long scales fringing their toes, helping them to walk on soft sand. Climbing lizards tend to have very sharp claws, which allow them to grip even smooth surfaces firmly. Some climbing lizards, such as geckos, have gripping pads on the soles of their feet as well. Webbed feet and paddle-shaped limbs are found on some aquatic turtles. For other swimming reptiles, such as crocodiles and monitor lizards, the tail provides most of the propulsion, and the limbs are folded back out of the way.

THE HARE AND THE TORTOISE
In the famous Aesop fable, the hare is so confident of winning his race with the slow and ponderous tortoise, that he falls asleep by the wayside, and the tortoise crosses the finishing line first. It is certainly true that although tortoises are slow, they make steady progress and can travel very long distances, seldom stopping for a rest.

LEGS OF ALL SORTS
The powerful feet and legs of lizards such as monitors and plated lizards are good for digging. The sharp-clawed toes of the girdled lizards give the animals a strong grip when climbing, often on flaking rock surfaces. The slightly webbed back feet of the crocodilians help propel them through the water. The limbs of the smaller skinks are so small that they barely support the animal.

Caiman

Plated lizard

Monitor lizard

African girdled lizard

Blue-tongued skink

All five toes spread out to achieve maximum grip

Geckos have no trouble moving vertically or hanging horizontally

GET A GRIP
The tokay, a fairly large gecko from eastern Asia, is so-called because one of the noises it makes sounds much like "tokay." This lizard is one of the best lizard climbers and has no difficulty scaling a wall, running across a ceiling, and even clinging to a sheet of glass. It grips by using pads on the underside of its fingers and toes. The pads are covered by microscopic, hairlike structures, which allow the gecko to cling to almost any surface. There may be as many as a million "hairs" on a tokay's pads, which rub the surface on which the animal is walking.

Elongated body resembles that of a snake

LOSS OF LEGS
This little glass lizard is often mistaken for a snake. It lives in rocky habitats or in thick vegetation. It has no front legs and only tiny, hardly visible remnants of back legs. These tiny back legs are called vestigial limbs, which are of little or no use to the animal. Many burrowing lizards have evolved in the same way. Without legs, these lizards can move around underground more easily.

Vestigial limbs are of no use in movement, but the male may use them in courtship to stimulate the female

LITTLE LIMBS
In most snakes, all traces of limbs have vanished. However, some of the more primitive groups, such as boas and pythons, have tiny remnants of the hip bones and hind limbs. The only external signs of these are small "claws" at the base of the tail, on either side of the vent, or anal opening.

Tokay gecko climbing

Ground control

MOST LIZARDS RELY ON SWIFTNESS and agility to hunt and to escape trouble. They usually use all four limbs and can move at high speed. Their legs and feet are specially adapted to where they live. Turtles have no need for speed. Instead, they have powerful legs, which can carry the extra weight of a protective shell and propel them forward slowly but surely. In spite of having no legs, snakes also move very efficiently on land in a variety of ways. Their method of movement may change depending on their surroundings. Crocodilians are most at home in water, but when on land they crawl, dragging their bellies along the ground. Occasionally, smaller crocodiles can "gallop."

LAND SPEED RECORD
The six-lined racerunner, a type of lizard found in North America, holds the record for the highest speed reached by a reptile on land, 18 mph (29 kph). This record was set in 1941 in South Carolina.

Palm flexed against the ground

Back legs provide most of the thrust

Tegu lizard

Long tail is used for balance

3 TWO AT A TIME
When a lizard breaks into a trot, its body is supported by two legs at a time (the diagonal pairs). There may even be times when both front feet and one hind foot are off the ground.

TWO LEGS ARE BETTER THAN FOUR
This crested water dragon comes from Asia and lives mainly in trees growing near water. If disturbed when on the ground, it may rear up on its hind legs and run along upright for short bursts, its tail helping it to balance. This type of bipedal (two-legged) locomotion is also displayed by other lizards. These lizards can achieve greater speed running on two legs than they can on four.

Alerted crested water dragon standing on all four paws

Lizard locomotion

Most lizards have four legs with five toes each, though there are some completely legless lizards and some with only tiny hind limbs. In most lizards, the back legs are stronger than the front and "power" the animal forward. Lizards that live underground often have much smaller legs or even none at all, as they tend to glide and wind through burrows, much like snakes.

1 PALM POWER
When this tegu lizard moves, the claws of its forelimbs point forward, "palm" down. The animal's forward thrust comes from the flexed "palm" pushing against the ground.

2 SIDE TO SIDE
When the lizard is going fast, it increases its stride by bending its body from side to side. The order in which the limbs are moved depends on how fast the lizard is traveling. When walking slowly, three feet are kept on the ground at all times.

Snake movement

Snakes use four main methods of getting around without legs: serpentine motion, concertina motion, sidewinding, and rectilinear motion.

NOW YOU SEE ME
A sidewinding Namib desert adder has been here. The snake lifts loops of its body clear of the surface as it moves sideways, leaving these distinctive barlike tracks. This method of movement keeps the snake from slipping when it is edging its way across a soft sand dune.

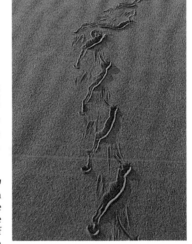

Sidewinding

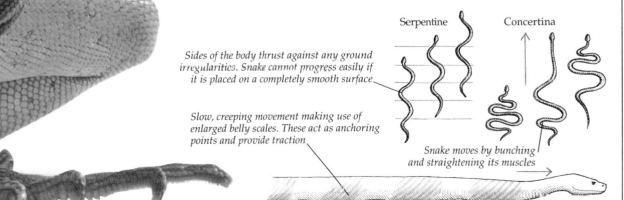

Serpentine   Concertina

Sides of the body thrust against any ground irregularities. Snake cannot progress easily if it is placed on a completely smooth surface

Slow, creeping movement making use of enlarged belly scales. These act as anchoring points and provide traction

Snake moves by bunching and straightening its muscles

Rectilinear

HIGHLY STRUNG

For much of the day, this mangrove snake lies high up in a tree. In the late afternoon or early evening, it slides into action, raiding nests for birds and their young. It is a rear-fanged snake, found in mangrove swamps and near rain forests.

Life in the trees

Many lizards and snakes are well adapted for life in trees and bushes. The toes of many arboreal or tree-dwelling lizards are often equipped with well-developed claws for gripping tree trunks, or special pads for clinging to smooth leaf surfaces. These lizards and some of the tree snakes often have long tails, which they twist around a branch, helping them to keep their balance. Some tree snakes have ridges on their belly scales, giving them additional gripping power. Arboreal reptiles are often found on isolated islands in the Pacific Ocean. It is believed they reached there on floating bits of vegetation.

FURRY FAT FLIER

Like flying reptiles, the little flying squirrel glides rather than flies, using the folds of skin between its limbs. A lightweight animal, it sometimes eats so much it is unable to fly.

HOT LIPS

This tree boa from South America has heat-sensitive pits in its lips so that it can find the roosting birds and bats on which it feeds. A stretchy body and strong tail make it particularly suited to this habitat. As it climbs, it reaches up and coils itself around a branch, hauling up the rest of its body as it goes.

Coils act as anchor

FLYING ACE

This flying gecko has skin folds along its sides, legs, and tail; it also has webbed feet. Together these act as a parachute when the lizard glides through the air. Like the flying dragons, it uses its abilities to get out of trouble or to swoop down on food. The skin color and texture make the gecko difficult to detect when it sits on tree bark.

HANGING ON
An emerald green tree boa catches a bird. The snake uses a branch to support itself as it makes the kill.

COOLING DOWN
The trinket snake from India is a part-time tree-dweller. In hot weather it stays on the ground, sheltering in termite mounds or under rocks. However, in cooler weather it prefers to move up into trees and bushes. Although harmless to humans, it can look very frightening if threatened, swelling its neck and vibrating its tail as it strikes.

Garden lizard

BLOODSUCKER
The garden lizard's body is much like a chameleon's, and its tail is very long and slender. It can change color rapidly, especially its head, which sometimes turns red. In fact, the lips of some species become so red that these lizards have been nicknamed "bloodsuckers."

DAREDEVIL DRAGONS
Flying dragons have the same gifts in the air as the flying geckos, only their "wings" are flaps of skin stretched over elongated ribs. The wings fold back along the sides of the animal when not in use.

DAY DUTY
All geckos are good climbers, as the pads with clinging hairlike projections on their toes allow them to tackle almost any surface. This gecko is fairly unusual in that it is active by day; most geckos are active at night. Although day geckos eat a variety of insects and soft fruit, some seem to like the nectar that they find in palm flowers.

Waterproofed

TAIL WALKING
If a crocodile is being chased, or if it is giving chase, it can move very fast, even leaping out of the water. This "tail walk," much like that of dolphins, demonstrates how graceful and at ease the animal is in water.

ALTHOUGH MOST REPTILES ARE land animals, several groups of reptiles live successfully in water. Crocodilians, a few lizards (such as the marine iguanas of the Galapagos Islands), some snakes (like the giant anaconda of South America), and terrapins and turtles all spend much of their lives submerged. Most reptiles have to return to dry land to lay their eggs, or the developing animal would drown. Some sea snakes, found mainly in the oceans around Asia, northern Australia, and the Pacific Islands, get around this problem by giving birth to live young that are immediately able to swim and come up for air. Different reptiles use their watery home in different ways: crocodilians swim, hunt, and cool off in it, and marine iguanas feed on algae growing on the submerged rocks.

SNORKEL SNOUT
When an alligator dives, special muscles and flaps close over the nostrils and ears. In calm waters it needs to keep only its nose disk above the surface. Another flap at the back of the throat stops the lungs from being flooded when the alligator opens its mouth under water. Its eyes are also waterproofed – in addition to well-developed upper and lower lids, they are protected by a transparent shield that covers each eye.

Eyes set high on the head

Caiman lies still in water as a defense against predators and in order to catch prey

Caiman

JESUS CHRIST LIZARD

When frightened, this little basilisk lizard, also called the Jesus Christ lizard, can walk on water. It drops onto the water from riverside trees and swiftly scuttles across the surface on its back legs. Its feet have very broad soles, and the fringe of scales on its toes helps to support it on the water. As the lizard loses speed, it sinks and will then continue on its way swimming.

Basilisk lizard

MONSTERS OF THE DEEP

Humans have always believed that deep waters house strange creatures. Even today, many people believe in the existence of a monster in Scotland's Loch Ness. The extraordinary appearance of some water reptiles probably accounts for the myths that have grown up about them over the centuries.

THE WET LOOK

People are not as well adapted to survival in the water as many reptiles. Unlike reptiles, our skin needs protection if we are going to survive the effects of cold temperatures.

SOFT BACKS

Water turtles generally have lower, more streamlined shells than land turtles and are therefore better suited to swimming. These soft-shelled turtles are the flattest of them all and have the perfect shape for hiding beneath the sand and mud on the bottom of their watery home (pp. 30–31). Unlike their land relatives, their feet have long toes that are joined by a fleshy web. This gives them extra thrust as they move through the water.

The speed of the basilisk allows it to run on the surface of the water

Nostrils lie just above water level

WATER BABY

This young caiman is very well adapted for life in the water. Its eyes, nostrils, and ears are set high on its head. In this way it can still see and breathe as it lies unseen in the water. This is an advantage when hunting prey, or coming to the water's edge to drink. Not surprisingly, the caiman, like all the other crocodilians, is a good swimmer. At high speed it tucks its legs and webbed feet against its sides and propels itself forward using its powerful muscular tail. The caiman depends on water to such an extent that if exposed to hot sun for too long without water available to swim in, it will die.

UNDERWATER BREATHING

All turtles have lungs, but aquatic turtles can also breathe through their skin and through the lining of the throat. Some can tolerate very low oxygen levels and can survive for weeks under water, but this little red-eared terrapin can last for no more than two or three hours without surfacing.

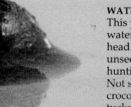
Red-eared terrapin

Best of enemies

REPTILES HAVE MANY NATURAL ENEMIES. Large birds, such as owls and eagles, and some mammals, such as hedgehogs, pigs, and cats, all prey on snakes and lizards. Some reptiles eat their own kind. Kingsnakes, found in the U.S. and Mexico, and the Asian king cobra are specialists in eating other snakes. Monitor lizards also frequently eat smaller reptiles. But reptiles' greatest enemies are humans. Crocodiles, snakes, and lizards are still killed for their skins. Snakes are also killed because they are so feared, and often captured live so their venom can be used for medical research (pp. 42–43).

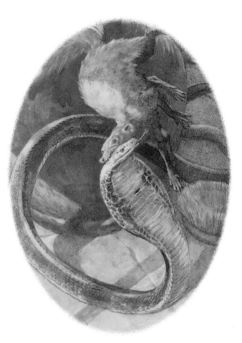

RIKKI-TIKKI-TAVI
In 1894, British author Rudyard Kipling wrote *The Jungle Book*, and created a hero of a little mongoose named Rikki-Tikki-Tavi. This little mammal lived with a British Family in India and became their protector, first killing Karait, a lethal krait snake, and then Nag, a cobra. The strength of the cobra is of little use to it once the mongoose has managed to grasp the back of the snake's head.

When the hood is extended, the "eye" is meant to terrify aggressors

ENEMY NUMBER ONE
One of the best-known enemies of many snakes, but in particular the cobra, is the mongoose. In any fight between a mongoose and a cobra, the mongoose is likely to be the victor. Its speed and agility help it avoid the lunges of the snake. The mongoose will dart in and bite the back of the snake's neck, or it may grab the back of the snake's head until the snake gives up the struggle. Mongooses were introduced into the West Indies in an attempt to reduce snake numbers. However, they themselves have become worse pests, attacking small animals and poultry.

Hood spread in attack

The snake's body is bunched, ready for attack

THE KING
Lions are known to prey on crocodiles, even adult ones. On land, the speed and power of the mammal are enough to overcome the more sluggish reptile, although the outcome might be very different in or near water.

Stiff hairs on the mongoose's back are raised to give added protection

Razor-sharp teeth attack the cobra at the back of the head

Body lightly poised on back paws for quick movement

FEET FIRST
The secretary bird scares up possible prey, such as snakes, by stamping its feet and flapping its wings. When a snake appears, attracted by the vibrations, the bird quickly kicks at it or stamps on it, at the same time covering the snake with its wings to keep it from moving into a position from which it can defend itself. In this way, it can even deal with dangerous snakes such as adders and cobras. If stamping does not kill the snake, then the bird will carry it high into the air and drop it onto hard ground.

WAR DANCE
In Indian mythology, the demon Kaliya changed himself into a cobra and killed many herdsmen in his search for the god Krishna. Finally, Krishna killed Kaliya and then danced on his head.

TARZAN TRIUMPHS!
Tarzan the apeman has no difficulty overpowering his reptilian enemy. In real life, a struggle between a crocodile and a human could have a very different ending. Although crocodiles are not usually man-eaters, they will certainly attack anyone foolish enough to stray near crocodile-infested rivers or breeding grounds.

Just good friends

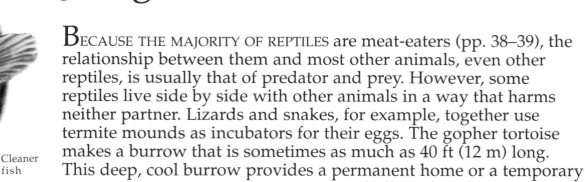

Cleaner fish

BECAUSE THE MAJORITY OF REPTILES are meat-eaters (pp. 38–39), the relationship between them and most other animals, even other reptiles, is usually that of predator and prey. However, some reptiles live side by side with other animals in a way that harms neither partner. Lizards and snakes, for example, together use termite mounds as incubators for their eggs. The gopher tortoise makes a burrow that is sometimes as much as 40 ft (12 m) long. This deep, cool burrow provides a permanent home or a temporary hiding place for many animals besides the tortoise. Other tortoise burrows have been found in which possums, raccoons, rabbits, lizards, and rats were living together happily. Even rattlesnakes are said to live peacefully with the other inhabitants in such a home.

A HELPING HAND

The tuatara's existence on the remote islands off New Zealand is largely made possible by sea birds such as petrels and shearwaters (pp. 36–37). In fact, the tuatara sometimes shares its burrow with these birds. They cover the rocks and ground with their droppings, creating a perfect environment for large numbers of insects, including beetles and crickets, the tuatara's favorite food. However, it is an uneasy relationship, as tuataras eat nestling birds instead of insects if they get the chance.

Tuatara

Shearwater

A FRIEND INDEED

The African helmeted turtles clean tiny parasites from hippopotamuses and rhinoceroses that enter their watering holes. This cleaning behavior is not uncommon. Some turtles are known to use their jaws to pull algae from other turtles' shells – and then they change places.

Hippopotamus

African helmeted turtle

THREE'S NOT A CROWD

All sorts of reptiles occasionally find themselves living side by side, often for different reasons. The hinge-back tortoise dislikes the dry weather of the African grasslands and hides from the hot sun in its burrow until the rainy season begins. The house snake investigates the same burrow for its favorite food, rats and mice, and the skink scuttles in to hide from an enemy. But it had better watch out. House snakes eat skinks if there is a shortage of rodents!

SLEEPING PARTNERS

Birds are sometimes said to pluck scraps of food and parasites from the gaping mouths of crocodiles. There is some doubt whether birds such as plovers would risk this, but it is true that some wander, apparently safely, among sleeping crocodiles. Some birds, such as the water dikkop, nest near crocodiles and are indirectly protected by, and protect, their fearsome neighbors. Few animals will attack the birds while the crocodiles are nearby, and the birds' noisy reaction at the approach of an enemy in turn acts as an early warning device to the reptiles.

CLEANING UP

Many animals outside the reptile world live in such a way that in helping others, they also help themselves. An amazing example is the cleaner fish. It picks parasites and fragments of food off bigger fish. Here a tiny cleaner is grooming a huge fish in Australia's Great Barrier Reef.

An eye to the future

Unless we change the way we live, many reptiles face extinction. Although it has taken over 150 million years for the once immensely varied reptiles to be reduced to just four groups, these now face a greater threat than ever before. The main cause for concern lies in the terrible destruction of their natural habitats. Many reptiles have specially adapted to life in some of the areas that are being lost at a frightening rate – for example the rain forests in the tropics and much of the shrubland of Europe. Although governments are now more aware of the situation and have agreed to help some severely threatened species, too little may have been done too late.

SOUP, SOUP, BEAUTIFUL SOUP
In some areas, reptiles are still very popular as a food for humans. Just a few years ago in the Caribbean 5,000 marine turtles were turned into 150,000 gallons (682,000 liters) of soup by just one food firm.

SAFE – FOR HOW LONG?
Although still fairly common, the giant skink of the Solomon Islands faces a problem shared by many other reptiles. Its habitat is being rapidly developed, and there is concern that as this happens many of these lizards will face extinction. This particular skink has further problems – it is commonly eaten in some areas. This very large animal spends nearly all its life in trees, as its monkey-like tail suggests. It eats mostly leaves and is active mainly at night.

TOURIST TRAP
This beautiful beach in Turkey is one of the last nesting sites of loggerhead turtles. Threatened by building development as a result of the tourist trade, these marine turtles face a very uncertain future, despite their long and varied history.

Baby big-headed turtle

BIG HEAD
The head of this turtle (well-named the big-headed turtle) is so large that it cannot be withdrawn into its shell. It is not yet acknowledged as being especially endangered, but because it looks so strange, it is often captured for the pet trade or used to make souvenirs. It lives in Southeast Asia, where during the day it spends its time buried in the gravel or under rocks in cool mountain streams.

An old engraving shows the head size in proportion to the body.

Dirty dealing

In some parts of the world conservationists are trying to save reptiles, but many animals are still slaughtered to provide skins for the leather trade and souvenirs for tourists – including key rings made from the heads of hatchlings. Thousands of other reptiles have been collected by the pet trade, although in a few instances successful captive-breeding programs have helped to maintain the existence of rare species (pp. 36–37).

Siamese crocodile head keyring

Rattlesnake boot

UNHAPPY PET

The Pacific Island boa is found in a variety of habitats on the Solomon Islands, such as forests, farms, and near human dwellings. Although primarily a ground snake, it climbs well and is sometimes found in tree hollows, living on young lizards, rodents, and birds. This snake is sometimes kept as a pet, which is unfortunate, because in captivity it often "sulks" and refuses to eat. However, like the giant skink, it is threatened mainly by a disappearing habitat.

DOWN THE LADDER

Snakes are probably disappearing faster then any other group of vertebrates. They are at greater risk than ever in the 20th century, constantly in danger of being run over by cars. If something is not done to protect their habitats soon, we may be left with only board games and decorative models to remind us of these amazing animals.

Bead snake made by prisoners of war in 1916

Index

Acknowledgments

Dorling Kindersley would like to thank:
Trevor Smith and all the staff at Trevor Smith's Animal World for their help and enthusiasm.
Cyril Walker at the Natural History Museum for pages 8 and 9.
Keith Brown, Isolde McGeorge, and Chester Zoo for their kind permission to photograph tuataras.

Picture credits

t=top b=bottom l=left r=right c=center

A.N.T./P & M Walton/N.H.P.A.: 10br; 56tl
Ancient Art & Architecture Collection: 34b
Aquila Photographics: 60ml
Ardea: /J.A. Bailey 22tr; /Jean-Paul Ferrero 48br
E.N. Arnold: 14bl
Biofotos/S. Summerhays: 23tr
Bridgeman Art Library: 26b; 62ml
British Museum (Natural History): 9m
Jane Burton: 25b
© Casterman: 40tr
Bruce Coleman Ltd: 33mr; /M. Fogden 7mr; /A. Stevens 7b, 42tr, 53br; /P. Davey 14mr, 38ml; /F. Lauting 19tr; /E. Bauer 19m; /D. Hughes 21b; /J. & D. Bartlett 28l; /C. Ott 33br; /J. Burton 38tl; /G. Zeisler 41ml; /B. Wood 42m; /J. Foote 42bc, 62tl; /R. Williams 46bm; /L. Lee Rue III 56tr; /M. Brulton 62-3t; /C. Frith 62t
Dorling Kindersley: 24m
Mary Evans Picture Library: 7tr; 8tl; 17tl;

18tl; 27tr; 38mr; 40mr; 43tl; 50-1; 57tm; 58tl
Sally & Richard Greenhill: 24mr
Robert Harding Picture Library: 14br; 16t; 47tl; 57mr
Michael Holford: 30tl; 34tr
Kobal Collection: 43tm
Frank Lane Picture Agency: 60m
Musee National d'Histoire Naturelle, Paris: 30ml
National Museum of Wales: 30mr
N.H.P.A.: 57ml; 61tm
Natural Science Photos: /P.H. & S.L. Ward 32
Oxford Scientific Films: 52tl; 61tl; /S. Osolinski 18m; /K. Atkinson 37br; /Z. Leszczynski 41mr, 46bl; /J. Gerlach 42bl; /Stouffer Productions 54m; /S. Mills 62br
Planet Earth Pictures: 60tl; 61br; /K. Lucas 20m; /P. Scoones 37tr
Ann Ronan Picture Library: 22bm
South Kensington Antiques: 62bc
Frank Spooner Pictures: 28br
Syndication International: 6ml
By Courtesy of the Board of Trustees of the Victoria & Albert Museum: 34m
Wildlight Photo Agency/Oliver Strewe: 21tr
Jerry Young: 42c, 43c

Illustrations by Andrew Macdonald:
13; 17; 21; 38; 41; 42; 47; 51; 53